Miriam Steiner-Avieze

THE SOLDIER WITH THE GOLDEN BUTTONS

Miriam Steiner-Aviezer

THE SOLDIER WITH
THE GOLDEN BUTTONS

Yad Vashem • Jerusalem • 1987

Translated by Miriam Arad

Originally published as "Vojak z zlatimi gumbi"
By Mladinska knjiga, Ljubljana, 1964
In Hebrew published by "Moreshet", Tel Aviv, 1977, 1988
In Serbo-Croate published by "A. Cesarac", Zagreb, 1980

Second edition, 2005

ISBN 965-308-224-8

Typesetting: Shulamit Yerushalmi, Jerusalem
Printed in Israel, 2005
by Daf Noy, Jerusalem

In memory of
my parents

Contents

Foreword

In 1946, at Crikvenica on the Adriatic Sea, the American Joint Distribution Committee organized a holiday camp for Jewish child survivors of the Holocaust. Nearly all the children had been in one or another Yugoslovian death camp. Its horrors were still fresh in their minds, and marked their entire conduct – the way they ate and walked and played on the beach.

But it was at night, in bed, that the past would come wholly alive, and it was then, in the darkness, that the children told one another their stories. I was one of those children, and I, too told my stories. What we all had in common was our inability to describe our feeling – even simply to say how we each loved our own Mama.

It is those stories, told a few months after the event, that I have combined in this book and made into the story of Biba.

The book was originally written in Slovenian, and first published in Ljubljana, Yugoslavia.

Jerusalem, 1987   Miriam Steiner-Aviezer

One

The last of the morning mist was lifting over the village. The shepherds were taking their flocks out to pasture, bearing baskets for the mushroom and blackberries that filled the woods at this time of year. The herd shuffled along, working its way between the village houses with a great bleating and tinkling of bells.

The little village was coming awake.

Curls of smoke rose over roofs, issuing from the chimneys in heavy puffs as though pushed by someone from below. Bedding appeared on the windowsills, followed by the heads of sleepy peasant girls leaning out over pillows and eiderdowns, calling to each other, exchanging first bits of gossip. Men went to draw water from the well, listen to their neighbours' morning news, and return to homes fragrant with coffee and fresh-baked bread.

The village was coming alive.

Young girls in wide newly washed skirts, an edge of starched petticoat showing, emerged into the road. Their numbers grew as they crossed the village and were joined by other girls, all on their way to the railway station. There, as on every other morning of the week, they would catch the train into town, bearing eggs and milk, cheese and cream and blackberries, and the early-summer smells of meadow and forest and farm. Last came the women toting washtubs and wooden scrubbing boards, going down to the river to sing and chatter and joke as they did their washing.

The big children were going off to school, the small ones heading for the slope below the mansion, and, as though by prior agreement, racing to the tracks to meet the morning train.

They could hear it coming in the distance – a cheerful whistle, then the engine itself appearing round the hill, a huge kindhearted monster rushing towards them. It blew a think cloud of smoke as it swept past, and gave a drawn out whistle as though greeting the children: "Hello there! See you tomorrow!" It pulled a string of cars behind it as lightly as cardboard boxes.

The children raced the train, laughing and waving and shouting "Godspeed!" till the last car had gone out of sight beyond the turning. The sound of its whistle faded, and still they stood by the tracks and gazed after the vanished train, thinking what it must be like to sit at one of those windows and speed past forest and villages and towns, on and on till you reached the Big City. There, in the city, you had smooth paved sidewalks of muddy pathways, tall, many-storied houses, tramcars and automobiles, shop-windows filled with toys and books and lovely clothes. They had agreed that if one of them should ever go on the train, all the other kids would wave to him till he'd be nothing but a tiny speck by the window.

The last trace of smoke and coal smell had blown away,

and at last the children turned from the track and started for the hillside near the river, their usual playground.

It was Maria's turn to preside over their games that day. It had just recently occurred to them to appoint a different "games monitor" each day, the way the big children had their class monitor at school. The child winning most of the day's games would be next day's monitor. It was a large new world, a new responsibility.

The monitor was in absolute command. He could invent new games, choose helpers if the game demanded it, and even decide not to play at all, in which case they were supposed to sit still all morning without doing anything. Biba was wishing they would play hide-and-seek. She had discovered the most wonderful hiding place where no one would find her, and was sure she would win. And then her great wish would come true: she would be monitor tomorrow.

Maria was taking her task very seriously. She frowned, scolded, issued commands: "Come here, everybody! You too, Mojca! Be quiet! You heard me, Breda! ...Listen: I've decided on two games for today. First we'll play hide-and-seek, and then prisoner's base."

"Hurray!" Biba shouted. "Hurray" was a new word she had only just learnt from her father, she felt very grown up using it,

"Why can't we play prisoner's base first?" Lucka demanded.

"Because I said so, and I'm in charge today. It's hide-and-seek first, and I don't want to hear another word about it. Come and be counted!"

They gathered round her, hands behind them, heads bowed, and Maria started counting, touching each head in turn:

"Air-bair, you are a hare. Og-bog, you are a hog..." Biba was terrified she would come out last and have to be It, so that when she was counted out the third time round she uttered a little shriek and skipped a few times round the Big Oak for joy. Breda was It; and just as she had gone to stand by the tree with her face in her hands, and as Biba was about to run to her new hiding place, a distant voice began calling: "Biba! Biba!"

Everyone turned to where the voice was coming from, and saw Toncek. Actually Toncek should have been at school, but he had stayed home that day because of a bad eye. They watched as he scampered downhill, arms flailing, then waited for him to catch his breath. Still panting, he turned to Biba and announced:

"You are wanted."

"Me? Why? It's not even lunch time yet. I don't want to go."

"You must. Your papa wants you."

"Papa?" she said, surprised. "Is my papa at home? Do we have visitors?"

"I guess so. Everybody's there. Hurry up."

It seemed a shame to Biba to have to leave just when she had such a chance to win.

"Please," she asked Maria, "couldn't you play prisoner's base till I'm back?"

"Oh, all right. Don't be long, though."

Biba set off at a run. After a few steps she turned to see whether Maria was keeping her promise, then ran on, satisfied. Swiftly she climbed the hill to the mansion, wondering who the unexpected visitor might be.

Could it be Uncle Zvonko? He does always turn up when no one's expecting him. Turns up just like that in his big motorcar with the funny-sounding horn that brings all the kids running. He generally has a nice present for her too. And takes all the kids on a ride through the village, with a great deal of noise and horn-honking. Very likely he's brought her that big doll with the black lace petticoat.

But maybe it isn't Uncle Zvonko at all? Maybe it's Grandma?

Oh, but if it is Grandma, then some preparation is called for. Biba stopped for a moment to check whether her nails were clean, her frock neat; wiped her muddy shoes on the grass, and walked on carefully stepping high, mindful of the instructions that preceded each of Grandma's visits. She could see herself come up the stairs to the large drawing room reserved for visitors and great occasions. She would keep her eyes half closed as she crossed the room, on account of the scary pictures on the walls, but take good care not to stray from the narrow red carpet leading straight up to Grandma's armchair. Grandma will be sitting there bolt upright, very likely dressed in the black lace blouse with stand-up collar, with Papa and Mama standing over her, answering questions. Biba will make a little curtsy like a ballerina, and Grandma will chuckle and open her arms wide. Then Biba, happy to have the formalities over, will climb onto Grandma's knees, hug and kiss her, chatter to her heart's content.

Biba loved Grandma very much. True, Grandma would often look awfully grim – she was stiff and severe, and moved about with difficulty – but Biba always felt that the frowning forehead and the grave eyes were just a cover for the smile underneath.

Grandma would tell her stories – always the same stories – but Biba could never quite follow them because she didn't know Grandma Language* very well. She always got bored halfway through, and never found out whether the prince did marry the princess, the witch punished and the children saved.

After the story would be the presents. Very likely it would be one of those little velvet boxes in which rings and brooches and lockets are kept. But even before Biba would get a chance to look inside, Papa would put it away in the large steel box which only he knows how to open, and Grandma would say in her language:

"You can wear it when you're big."

Next Grandma would want to take a stroll through the garden to see whether the seedlings she and Biba planted are blooming. Biba would fetch the walking stick, and would be rewarded by another kiss on her forehead.

They say that once upon a time Grandma was a little girl herself, that she fought with other kids, threw stones, climbed trees, played hide-and-seek, yelled, giggled. That's what they say, but Biba knows what is true.

She reached the mansion before she could make up her mind whether it was Uncle Zvonko or Grandma – and pulled up with a start.

* German

The whole village was there: Aunt Lizinka, the servants, the peasants, everybody. They all stood there and listened to Papa who, very pale in the face, was explaining something to them with his arm around a moaning and weeping Mama. For a moment Biba just stared at them, amazed and a little fightened. What in the world could have induced Papa to come out of the house bareheaded and coatless, and to stand there before strangers with his suspenders showing, and embracing Mama for all to see!

Biba approached uncertainly. All at once people spotted her, and a whisper went through the crowd: "There, there is Biba now."

How strange that they should take so much notice of her.

Now Mama rushed over, scooped Biba up in her arms and began kissing her with lips that were all wet and salty:

"Oh my little Biba, what harm have you ever done? Oh, God – why? Why?"

"Mama?" whispered Biba, alarmed, but as Mama still didn't stop crying, Biba began to wipe away Mama's tears, hugging and kissing and trying to comfort her, on the point of tears herself.

Papa joined them. He kissed the top of Biba's head, then let them both inside, talking to Mama all the time, saying "Hush, Zora, calm down, we've got to be sensible now, we have only one hour left."

Upset as she was, Biba still realized it was the first time she had ever heard Papa call Mama by her name; and that, as much as anything, convinced her that something unusual had happened.

Inside the house, Aunt Lizinka took her from Mama and

handed her over to Francka the servant girl, and together they went to the kitchen. Biba climbed up on her chair, and sat staring ahead of her – thinking, trying to make some sense of what was happening round her. Why in the world was everyone crying? Why was Francka here rubbing her face with a corner of her apron and wandering about the kitchen as if she were a stranger in it?

Biba watched her in silence for a while, before venturing her question.

"Francka," she said carefully, "what happened? Why is everyone crying?"

For reply Francka burst into tears again and Biba settled down resignedly to wait. She was quite familiar with the sight of Francka in tears. Francka would weep if someone praised her cake, if the church choir sang well on a Sunday; she wept at good news, and all the more at bad. She wept all the time, as though she knew no other way to express her feelings.

Today was different, though. Today it wasn't just she. Today Aunt Lizinka wept, and the peasant women, and everyone. Today Mama wept.

Francka placed a bowl of soup before her, but Biba folded her hands resolutely behind her and sat back in her chair.

"I won't eat unless you tell me why everyone is crying."

"It's because we're sorry you're going away."

"Who's going away?"

"You, Biba. You and your ma and dad."

"Why? Away where?"

"On a trip."

"On a trip? But where?"

"Far away, lovely, ever so far away..."

There were ominous signs of fresh outburst, and Biba, afraid it would put an end to this fascinating conversation, hurriedly went on:

"Yes, but where? On a trip where?"

"Dunno. I just know it's far away."

"On a trip."

"Mm."

"On a train?"

"Sure on a train. What else?"

Biba thought at once of that morning's train, and of how they agreed that if one of them should go away on it, all the others would stay by the track and wave as long as they could. And now she would be behind one of those windows, waving to all her friends till she'd be nothing but a tiny speck, till the train would be lost out of sight round the hill. Would she really be the first to travel on the train then? Or was Francka just saying it to cheer her up, make her eat? Biba put on a stern, searching expression.

"Are you telling me the truth, Francka? Will I really be going on a train?"

"Cross my heart!"

"I'll go on a train," Biba repeated to herself dreamily. "On a proper train, a big train... Is that why you're crying, Francka? But Francka, it isn't dangerous at all! You could even come with us yourself. Shall I ask Papa if you can?"

"On duckie, I'd sure go with you if I could. I'd go anywhere with you..." Here she broke down again, and Biba tried to comfort her:

"Don't cry, Francka! Look, I'm going to finish all my

soup, and... I'll never lick off the cream off your cake again, and never-ever scare the chickens..."

But that just seemed to make Francka ever more unhappy. She cried louder at every word, till in the end she sank on a chair, dropped her head in her arms and sobbed so hard that the table shook. Biba thought it would scarcely be polite to go on eating now, and considered it her duty to console Francka. But then Francka jumped up suddenly as though she remembered something important, and began hurrying to and fro in the kitchen – packing food into a hamper. In that case, they must really be going on a trip.

Sure of her facts now, Biba began eating fast, the sooner to go and give her friends the happy news.

Aunt Lizinka came into the kitchen. Biba was about to ask her whether she knew they were going on a trip, but the sight of her wet face stopped her. Aunt Lizinka changed Biba's clothes, then knelt to put her shoes on for her. Biba sat and watched the tears trickling slowly down her face; They no sooner welled up in her eyes than they ran over and down her cheeks, and new tears formed. Funny things, tears. Where did they come from, anyhow? But she had no time to go into that now. She must hurry to the entrance hall to say goodbye to everyone.

All the servants were there. And there was Ivica, too, appearing at a run, quite out of breath, her long braids all dishevelled, and her face – always full of laughter – showing no trace of merriment now. She stared at Biba with wide, stricken eyes, opened her mouth to say something, and then closed it again. Other people had turned up, too, friends of Papa's: the judge, the doctor, the teacher, the notary, even the priest; other villagers, ladies. Many of them were crying. It occurred to Biba that she herself was no doubt expected to cry too. The trouble was that she didn't know how to turn on that mysterious tap. She rubbed her eyes and screwed up her face as she kissed people goodbye, and made everyone think she was really crying. All the while she was longing to see her friends. No doubt they already knew and were waiting for her by the Big Oak.

Presently she saw her chance and slipped out -- there they all were, in front of her house! She began calling to them from afar:

"I'm going, going on a train!"

She told them again at close quarters, her voice shrill with excitement: "I'm going on the train! On the train!" She repeated it several times, for they seemed not to grasp it: they stood there in silence, not answering, just staring at her.

"Didn't you hear me? I'm going away on the train – the big train with the engine. You will have to stand by the tracks and wave to me like we said."

And still they said nothing, weren't glad, didn't protest, only stood and looked silently at Biba.

"Don't you hear what I'm saying? I'm going away? We're to leave in just a little while. Everything's ready, food and things, and in just a little while we'll go, and I'll be on the train... What presents shall I bring you from my trip?... But you don't have to tell me – I know. For you, Toncek, a gun to shoot sparrows with; for Breda – a doll with real hair and a silk dress; for Mojca – a huge box of chocolates in silver paper; for Maria – a picture book; and for you, Lucka... either cookie cutters or a teddy bear that cries. Right, and now we must say goodbye..."

She drew near, put her hand out, but none of them made to return the gesture. They even seemed to back away a little. She looked at them, bewildered.

"What's the matter with you? Why do you just stand there and stare at me? Say something! Why are you staring at me?"

Then Toncek asked abruptly: "Is it true that you're Jewish?"

Jewish? What was that? Why should she be Jewish? What did it mean, anyhow? No one had ever called her that. "Biba," they'd always call her, not "Jewish". "Darling Biba," yes, and sometimes "naughty Biba" or "stubborn Biba," but never "Jewish". Maybe she had got it wrong?

"What did you say, Toncek?"

"I say you're *Jewish*."

"Jewish?"

"Yes, Jewish."

"I'm not! I'm not Jewish ever!"

"Yes, you are!" Breda shouted. "You liar! You're Jewish, and so's your papa and mama! Everybody says so."

They were all shouting at her now, all her friends, and regarding her with aversion, hostility. "You're lying!" they shouted, and Biba looked at them, hurt and puzzled. Why in the world did they say she was lying, that she had *always* been lying, deceiving them, never letting on how she had been something else all along, and not just Biba? But what was this other thing? What could it be? What did it mean: Jewish? She supposed it must be something really horrid if it could turn them all against her like that, make them look at her as though she weren't one of them any more.

And then all at once they broke away, scattering like startled birds.

A soldier was standing in front of her. Young, tall, carrying a gun. A real gun, like the Uncle Zvonko took hunting. Biba looked at him as at a slightly unusual but passing phenomenon, nothing to do with her.

Here was Papa, too. He came and sat on his heels before her, put his hands on her shoulders, and she could tell he was going to say something very important.

"Listen, Biba," he began. His voice was low and gentle, but Biba caught the note of urgency in it. "You're a big girl, and you know there are things we must do whether we like it or not. Well, do you see this soldier here? He won't hurt you, and you needn't be afraid of him, but he's going to be with us all the time from now on. You are to do exactly as he tells you, and you are to stay close to us all the time. You'll give Mama a hand, and do as we say. All right?"

"All right," said Biba gravely, aware that for some unfathomable reason she would have to remember every word Papa had just spoken.

They were walking downhill, followed by the soldier. Behind the soldier came everyone else – the servants, Mama's and Papa's friends, the peasants, the kids. Their procession kept growing with every field they passed, people coming up to find out what had happened. Biba's friends ran on ahead, overtaking everyone so as to get to the railway station first, take up their post by the gate, as always when someone from the village was being seen off.

They arrived. The soldier would let only Aunt Lizinka and Francka come out to the platform with them, and made all the others stay behind the gate. Biba knew every corner, every bench at the station. She could point out the large warehouses, the post office, the waiting room, the stationmaster's office; she knew where the freight cars and the passenger coaches stood, and how the barrier was lowered. The only novelty today was the flag on the roof. She had never seen it before: a strange black flag.

The train had already pulled in, and the soldier made them board it right away, giving them no time to say goodbye. They mounted the high step and pulled the door behind them at once and ushered them to a compartment. Down there on the platform under their window, Aunt Lizinka and Francka stood weeping, and all the others watched them from behind the gate. Nearly the whole village was there, a few latecomers hurrying to join them even now. Biba kept her eyes on her friends, who were up in front, leaning on the gate.

Aunt Lizinka was trying to say something, and Biba struggled with the window, but the train began to move before she could raise it. Mama jumped up, stood with both palms pressed flat against the glass, her lips moving. Biba felt a bit troubled herself: were they going away just like that, without a proper leave-taking? Aunt Lizinka and Francka were moving with the train, running alongside as though they had just remembered they wished to come too and were running to catch up with it. They called out something, but their voices were drowned by the noise of the wheels. Biba waved. She leaned out of the window – she had managed to raise it at last with Papa's help – calling her friend's names, but they stood by the gate – motionless, not answering her, not racing the train, not waving. The train gathered speed, but still Biba waved, hoping that at least one of them would raise a hand in farewell.

The train approached the turning. "So, long!" she shouted as hard as she could, but she knew they could no longer hear her.

The train sped along, and before Biba could collect her thoughts, tell herself she was really traveling now, the village was lost to sight, station and children left far behind, only forests and hills beyond the window now.

Biba settled herself in her corner. Why hadn't they waved at her? They had agreed, hadn't they? How could they just have stood there by the gate, watching her in silence? Not given her a hand, not said "Goodbye" or "Godspeed"; and when little Lizzy had moved to race the train, Maria had stopped her. Why? Why ever?

No doubt Papa could have explained it all, but he was busy – giving Mama some pills and trying to comfort her. Why was Mama crying? What was making her so unhappy? What were they whispering about all the time? Why did Papa keep saying: "Zora, calm down, Zora"? She had never seen Mama so unhappy. Come to think of it, she had never before seen her cry. She felt like crawling into Mama's arms to console her, wipe her tears away.

Maybe it would help if she told her that she herself, Biba, was also feeling unhappy on account of the kids not waving and no one saying "Godspeed" or "So long". Ah, but she'd show them. She'd give them a piece of her mind when she came back! Or rather – she wouldn't. She would bring them presents, and then they would feel bad about not waving. She would bring each of them a present, just as she had promised. Papa was sure to give her some money. He always brought presents to his friends when he'd been away on a trip. She turned to look at him now: he was stroking Mama's hair, fanning her face with a piece of cardboard, and looking as if he didn't know quite what to do.

"Papa, where are we going?" The question came out so suddenly that she was a bit surprised herself.

Papa said nothing, which was unusual: as a rule he would answer her questions right away. Maybe he hadn't heard? She was about to repeat it when he said – very softly so as not to wake up Mama who had dozed off with her head on his shoulder: "We are going to see Aunt Ksenija."

"Really?" said Biba. "Then can I ride Vid's bike?"

"Sure you can."

Mama opened her eyes, smiled and held out her arms. Biba rushed into them, hugging Mama hard, delighted to see her happy again. Mama began to tell her about all they would see in the Big City, where they would go, what they would buy, whom they would visit. Then Biba told Mama about the presents, and what she had planned to bring each child, and Mama said better leave out the chocolate as it might go soft on the way. Papa promised to give her money, and Biba felt glad all over. Everything was all right again: Mama wasn't crying any more, they had stopped their whispering, they were talking to her as always, and Mama had even laughed once. She kissed each of them in turn and went to look out of the window.

Tall trees grew along the tracks, moving backwards fast, as though in a hurry to get somewhere. The more distant trees looked as if they were constantly changing places with each other, as in a game of musical chairs. Swallows sat on the telegraph wires, and the longer she looked at them the surer she felt that there wasn't any wire there at all, that the swallows were sitting on air. Miraculous, but possible. Ivica, whom she would often accompany to the pasture, had told her that birds, and especially swallows, could even *stand* in the air. They probably had to when they flew south and found nowhere to rest.

Now they were passing a small stream. Could it be the same one that flowed through their own meadow? Very likely it had found a shortcut and had overtaken them. Or maybe it ran underground? She'd been told that rivers could flow under the ground as well. But already they had left it behind, and now here was a field with sheep and cows, driven by a girl with long plaits, just like their Ivica. Look, she was running after the train and waving. Nice of her to do that. But the train hurried on, and far away in the distance you could already discern a new village approaching fast. Smoke curled up from the low red roofs, just as in their own village. The people in the fields looked up, leaning on their spades as though glad of the chance to give themselves a little rest. The cows mooed, the children raced the train and waved to her. Everyone was playing with her, everyone was hurrying – and she, Biba, outran them all, waving to them as though they were all her friends. Oh, she would have this train ride go on and on.

She fell to watching the wheels, their swift revolution. She whispered in rhythm:

"Clickety-clack, here-I-go;
clickety-clack, here-I-go,
clickety-clack, far – away;
clickety-clack, darling train."

She felt grateful to the whole world: to the smoke, the engine, to its hoarse whistle calling out to people, to the children, the fields, the woods, the villages. She was thanking them all, waving and crying: "So long! So long!"

She gave a start as someone seized her roughly from behind.

It was the soldier. He was ordering her back to her seat with a stern gesture. She crept onto her mother's lap and hid her face in Mama's coat. The soldier sat on the other side, right across from them, and looked at her. Biba looked back. With only one eye, to be sure, but looking at him all the same, and he noticed it all right. Biba decided to stare him down – and she won. The soldier blinked, turned his head and pretended to look out of the window. At that Biba's courage returned. She freed herself from Mama's coat and began to contemplate the soldier.

It was funny, actually: he had a gun and jackboots and a soldier's uniform, he could threaten and scowl, but Biba wasn't in the least afraid of him. He was young, and seemed awfully proud of his gun, which he kept adjusting against his shoulder. He rocked in his seat just like Biba, and just like Biba he was jolted and thrown back whenever the train stopped. Why fear him then?

They were approaching the station. Tall buildings began to appear, and the buses, tramcars. The train slowed down as it rolled past passenger and freight cars, which looked quite forlorn standing there without their engines. Biba longed to return to her window, but the soldier was motioning for them to get ready.

Mama dressed her, rearranged the food in the hamper, and seemed on the point of tears. In a moment she was really crying again, with her head on Paps's shoulder.

Papa was using his sensible voice on her: "But Zora, listen, they can't drive us out just like that. I'm sure it's just a mistake. You'll see, it'll be cleared up as soon as we get there. A mistake, a slip-up, you'll see."

They began whispering in Grandma Language, and Biba used the occasion to have a peek out the window and watch the big wheels of the engine come gradually to a halt, sniffing and snorting as though short of breath. Then a cloud of steam hid the view, and the soldier came and lowered the window. He moved to the exit, and stood patiently waiting there for them to conclude their preparations and join him.

The platform was crowded. Nearly everyone was carrying suitcases, and many people were hugging and kissing one another – some because they were going away, and some because they had just arrived. One man ran after a moving train, and Biba paused to see if he would make it, but the soldier gave her a push – so rudely that she stuck out her tongue at him. He pretended not to have seen, and Biba left it at that: she had not time for getting cross with the soldier now, there were too many things to be seen. There was, for instance, a row of small wooden huts selling lemonade, chocolate, sweets, cigarettes, picture postcards, books, newspapers, toys – just like little shops.

A young fellow in a white jacket was crying "Lemonade! Orangeade! Sandwiches! Cakes!..."

A woman's voice announced over a loudspeaker: "The train from Zagreb is arriving at Platform Two."

One old man had an enormous sort of bag hanging from his neck and coming all down his front. The bag was full of newspapers, and he was waving one in his hand very excitedly and shouting about someone having been killed somewhere, and houses having been destroyed, and war.

There were large posters up on the walls and columns. One poster showed a cheerful looking man drinking beer and one eye shut in a wink. In another, a pretty but mournful lady was holding her head on one hand and gazing at some pills in the other. A third picture had a little girl with curls and a blue frock drinking a glass of milk. Most of the pictures, though, were of a uniformed man with a moustache who was yelling and shaking his finger threateningly.

There were many soldiers about as well, with guns and jackboots, but they were hurrying to the train like everyone else, which seemed perfectly natural to Biba. Some soldiers were seen off by women, like regular people.

Biba wanted to ask Papa why the man in the picture was yelling and shaking his finger so, but he was talking softly to Mama and she didn't want to interrupt.

They were led to some office, and the first thing that met them was the same picture of the yelling man with the moustache again. It hung on the wall facing the door, above a desk with a young officer seated behind it. Papa went over and started explaining to him in a very polite sort of way, with Mama putting a word in now and then. What puzzled Biba was that Papa was talking to an absolute stranger in Grandma Language, and that Mama was even helping him do it. They were trying to convince the officer of something, no doubt something very important because they were showing him all sorts of papers. He wasn't listening to them, though. He was busy trying to raise the lid of an inkpot on the far side of his desk with the help of the thin stick in his hand. The stick went up and down, each time just disturbing the lid, but whenever it seemed to just tip it up – the lid dropped shut again. The officer did not give up, though. He frowned, concentrated, tried again, till in the end he succeeded. He glanced round satisfied, as though expecting applause, then put his stick on the desk and looked up at Mama and Papa, as though surprised to find there were people in the room.

For a while he pretended to listen to what they were saying, but Biba felt he was just shamming, trying to make himself important. He sat watching them calmly, almost amiably, but all of a sudden he jumped up, struck the desk with his stick and began screaming in Grandma Language.

Biba drew back. She had always thought of Grandma Language as one that could only be spoken softly, in a nice polite, dignified sort of voice – and here he was yelling and screaming and spitting and threatening, and very likely using ugly words too, because Mama moved further away from the desk as though his words were hurting her. Papa's hand with the papers fell to his side, and he put his arm around Mama without a word.

Biba gave the officer a defiant look, and for a moment she wished she were a boy, a big boy, to grab his stick and teach him how to behave. Oh, she would have shown him, the stuck-up beast. She was afraid Mama would cry again, and prayed hard she wouldn't because she would not have him see Mama's tears. But Mama did not cry. She was holding fast onto Papa, who stood and stared blindly ahead of him.

A few soldiers came in by a side-door, ushered them into a sort of cubicle behind the office, handed Mama a small box, explained something and sat down, prepared to wait.

Mama began taking things out of the box – a needle and thread and some rags. She stared at them, turning them over and over with a stunned look on her face, then showed them to Papa. Papa winced and shut his eyes like someone being suddenly stabbed by a large needle. Mama put a hand on his shoulder. For a moment, they just stood there, and then they suddenly threw their arms about each other and embraced as if saying goodbye. Mama recovered first. She picked up the rags, which Biba could now see were actually some bits of yellow fabric, and began sewing them onto the sleeves of their coats. Biba, was waiting impatiently for Mama to be finished with hers.

"Oh, it's a star!" she exclaimed. "Did you get one, too, Papa?"

"Yes darling, I did, and Mama did too."

"It's a very pretty one, isn't it?"

"Yes, very pretty."

The soldiers got up, led them back to the platform, and from there out into the street.

Biba discovered that many passers-by were looking at her. Pleased, she turned the arm with the star a little so that it would be visible to as many of them as possible and she even boasted of it in passing to one little girl, whispering: "Look at my star!"

They arrived at a huge courtyard with a building at one end of it. The yard was filled with military trucks, each one the size of a little house; large packing cases; huts with sentries in them; and hundreds of soldiers who were standing about in groups and apparently waiting for something. Everyone talked Grandma Language – Mama, Papa, the soldiers – and all at once it seemed to Biba that everyone else was talking properly and only she wasn't.

Papa and Mama entered the building, and Biba waited outside. She settled herself on top of a crate, but as she couldn't see very well from there, she climbed up on a taller one to obtain a good view of whatever might be going on in the courtyard.

Someone blew a whistle, and all the soldiers rushed over to the center of the yard, and in no time formed themselves into several long straight rows. For a while they stood still, then they turned and began marching like proper soldiers – all through the courtyard and out.

Now only one soldier remained. At first he just stood, stiff and straight like a statue, but soon he apparently grew bored and began marching up and down the yard. Biba studied him: there was something funny about him, but she couldn't put her finger on it. Then he turned full-face towards her, and she realized what it was. It was his tummy, which was round and heavy and bulging all over his trouser-belt. He was big and strong, but still looked more like a fat woman than a soldier. Rather like Heda, their neighbor. Yes, but Heda had a baby in her tummy. And he? What did he have? A baby, too perhaps? Well, she didn't see why not? Why shouldn't he have a baby in his tummy?

She might give him some of her chocolate. Better wait till he came nearer, though. Now the soldier saw her. He seemed astonished, as though asking himself where in the world *she* had come from, then gave her a good-natured grin. He marched on, glanced back at her over his shoulder once to send her a playful wink, then vanished behind a large truck. Certain he would reappear before long, Biba took out her chocolate bar; she would give him half as soon as he came back to her. He was nice, with his tummy and all, and he seemed ready to make friends with her. Never mind if he had a baby or not, she'd give him some chocolate anyhow. Better give it to him on the sly, though, as maybe soldiers weren't allowed to eat chocolate.

And here he was, her soldier, smiling and cheerful and all set to play with her. Biba held out her hand with the chocolate, but then the soldier caught sight of the star on her sleeve, turned on his heel and marched quickly away. Biba looked over her shoulder to see what had startled him so, but at that instant Mama and Papa came back. She slipped down from her perch and ran to meet them:

> "Where are we going now?"
> "To Aunt Ksenija."
> "Splendid!"

Biba liked saying "splendid". It was what Papa said when

he felt good about something, and Mama had adopted it too. When, for instance, she would see him from afar, walking home hat in hand, stopping to joke with a child, chat with a neighbor, she would announce that Papa was in a "splendid mood".

Now Biba wondered why the soldiers were coming along to Aunt Ksenija, too. Did that mean that they would always be with them from now on? Not that she was afraid of them. She had already got quite used to having them always about. They did keep their hands on their guns all the time, to be sure, but where would a soldier keep his hands if not on his gun? Not in his pockets, surely.

Two

When they reached Aunt Ksenija's, the soldiers gave Papa some order and left.

Biba was just thinking whether Aunt Ksenija would greet them again with her ritual cry of: "Lord, how big she's grown!" – when her aunt appeared and did just that. Vid was there, too, all got up in long trousers, white shirt and bow-tie, and looking like a copy of his father in miniature. He did give her a hand, but with such a disdainful look on his face that she felt obligated to pinch him at once. She didn't really want to fight with him just yet, for she had too many things to tell him, but she couldn't resist the urge.

They rarely met, Vid and she, but when they did they spent most of their time together quarrelling.

Vid discovered her star before she could show off about it, and made her tell him everything right away. Aunt Ksenija had bought her a bike, so new it was still in its wrappings, and Biba wanted to try it out at once. Now she wouldn't have to beg Vid to let her ride his any more. They went out into the yard, each on his own bike, Biba teasing Vid by racing away and forcing him to shout across the whole courtyard: "And what happened then?"

"And then everyone wept. I didn't, but I pulled a face and everyone thought I was really crying."

They took another turn round the yard, and when they met again Biba resumed her story:

> "And then we went on the train, and that was splendid. You've no idea how splendid riding on a train is."
>
> "As if I'd never been on a train!"
>
> "I know you have."
>
> "Yes, and on a ship, too, and even on an aeroplane!"
>
> "Really? Is that splendid?"
>
> "Nothing special."
>
> She detested those know-it-all airs of his. Nothing special indeed! She rode away from him shouting angrily:
>
> "But you've never been on a horse, so there!"
>
> "All right, all right," he said, yielding. "So let's hear the rest of it."

So Biba told him about the funny scene at the station, with everybody hugging and kissing and rushing about with suitcases, and how everyone had talked Grandma Language, and how her mama hadn't been pleased with the stars at all. Then she told him about a soldier with the baby in his tummy, and Vid had called her silly goose for not knowing that only ladies can have babies in their tummies, and that of course hurt Biba's feelings and she refused to say another word.

Supper was a silent affair. Vid's father didn't tell funny stories, and Aunt Ksenija didn't keep saying the food was there to be eaten, and to help themselves. The servant girl with the snails on her ears came and went with the dishes and nobody spoke. Then Mama burst out crying suddenly, for no reason at all, and Biba knew it would be very bad manners to ask for another helping of strawberries and cream just now, and the girl removed them. Having guessed what she had in mind, Vid sniggered behind his napkin, for which she took proper revenge of him under the table.

Things improved vastly in the bedroom. Papa and Mama were all cheerful again. They undressed her, played with her, and even allowed her to forgo her glass of milk. They put her between them in their big double bed, and she told them stories – all the stories *they* had told *her* when she was little – till late in the evening.

She felt certain she would dream that night, and sure enough: she was picking blackberries. Funny ones – with cream. Vid was there, too, but he was so clumsy that even little Lizzy, who had covered all her front teeth with silver paper, was laughing at him. Biba slipped off to her new hiding place, which she knew to be teeming with berries, but instead of berries she found children there – her friends, all her friends. They were up in the tree, riding the branches, and as she looked at them they seemed to turn into branches themselves. They were staring back at her without recognition. Suddenly there was a wolf there. He wore jackboots and had a gun, and he was yelling and shaking his finger at her. She wanted to run away but her feet wouldn't move, as if some witch were holding them fast under the ground. A face appeared above her. Aunt Lizinka. No, Aunt Ksenija, putting on her shoes for her. Behind her stands a soldier, and behind him another, and another – popping up one after the other, each bigger than the one before. The first soldier keeps still, and all the rest jump over him like in a game of leapfrog. Now there are soldiers all round her. Papa is standing in the doorway, half dressed: he has put his trousers on over his pajamas and his suspenders are showing. He keeps trying to explain something to the soldier, but he won't listen. Now the soldier seizes Papa, pushes him out. Another soldier is holding Mama, but she struggles free, makes for the door, calls out, all in tears: "Don't part us! Please let us stay together... Bela! Be-la-a-a!" She stumbles, falls, you can see the bare soles of her feet coming out of her night-dress. Two soldiers pull her to her feet, and drag her out. She tries to resist, waves her hands about, screams. Someone stops her mouth with his hand. Above it her eyes show wide, streaming with tears. Now a solder is coming for Biba. The nearer he gets to her, the fatter he looks. Maybe it's the one with the big tummy. Biba wants to hide, but she can't move, like before with the wolf. The soldier bundles her up in a blanket, picks her up, carries her slung over his shoulder like a sack. In this odd position she catches sight of Vid. Even in his pajamas and without his glasses on he still looks like his father. Behind him is Aunt Lizinka. No, Aunt Ksenija. She is crying. The girl with the snails appears too, but only for a moment. And then it seems as if no one is holding her any longer, as if she is flying through the air, but out in the street, breathing cool night air. She bumps against something hard, and now the ground under her starts moving, and she is slipping on a moving floor and has nothing to hold on to. There are soldiers round her, sitting on both sides of her. Their black boots are like a wall, and Biba rolls over against them, trying to regain her balance. The guns behind their grim faces are topped with glittering bayonets. In front of her is the darkness, approaching, bringing fear with it. It is coming nearer, nearer, closing in on her, she can feel its fingers, in a moment it will pounce...

A distant, muffled cry reached her ears: "I want my child!"

Biba started, cried "Mama!" – and all at once it dawned on her: she was not asleep, not dreaming, but riding in a truck, surrounded by soldiers, all by herself, without Mama. They had abducted her. They were taking her away.

She crouched in a corner. The truck pulled up with a jolt, knocking her over. Fear choked her. Someone picked her up, lifted her out of the truck. The moment she felt solid ground under her feet she broke out running, faster and faster, not knowing where – anywhere so long as it was away from the soldiers. Her ear caught the familiar voice:

"I want my child, my child! Biba!"

"Mama, Mama, Mama-a-a!" Biba shrieked, running, making for the voice, willing Mama to hear her over the whistle of the train, the cars, the crying women. She fought her way through jackboots, suitcases, trucks, wagons, crates – running at the voice which was still hoarsely crying: "Biba! Bi-b-a-a!"

And then she saw her. Two soldiers were holding her arms, dragging her by the hair – dragging her with a crowd of other women to the open door of a railway car.

"Mama!" she screamed, gripped by a wild panic, overwhelmed by a sense of impending disaster.

"Bi-ba-a-a!" she heard the voice, very near now, here, right over her head. Then Mama saw her, too. And Mama clung with one hand to the doorframe and put out the other at Biba – and was gone.

At that instant someone seized Biba roughly by the hair and lifted her up. She screamed, hit out wildly, bit, kicked, demanded to be put down. She felt herself being carried through the crowd, being carried further and further away from where Mama had vanished. And here was the train once more, the wide open door, just like the one through which Mama had vanished. She felt a glimmer of hope: maybe they were taking her to Mama? But then she was flying through the air once more, and in a moment she struck a hard iron surface.

A sharp pain went through her head. Alarmed, feeling as if her whole head were swelling up, worried that something would grow on her forehead, she pressed both hands against her head, closed her eyes, and a thousand little pictures flashed through her mind – mingling and fading into each other: Vid without his glasses, Mama between the two soldiers, the soldier with the tummy, the yelling man with the moustache and the finger... To escape the pictures she opened her eyes again, fixed them in the darkness. The wooden floor she was sitting on gave a sudden lurch and began to move, and she felt the throb of wheels under her. Was she traveling then? On a train? Yes, on a train. Being taken away. *Sent away*. And Mama?

She leapt to her feet, began to shout, "Open up! Open up!" savagely beating her fists against the door of the accelerating car.

"Open up!" she shrieked, frantic with the horror of being taken away, further and further away from Mama.

The train was thundering along at full speed now.

"Open up! Open up!" Her voice echoed back at her from the walls, repeating in chorus: "Open up, open up..."

"Open up, open up..." her voice weakened, faltered. She slumped to her knees, fear flooding her, pressed her face against the door, knew only that whatever happened, she must not turn round.

There was something behind her. What? An abyss? A monster? A soldier with a stick? A wild beast?

Now it moved. She flattened herself against the door, petrified. Then with a sudden resolve, nerving herself, she swung round.

It was quite near, facing her now. In a moment it would touch, stick its claws into her.

She shut her eyes, resigning herself to her fate, motion-less, waiting for what seemed an eternity. Nothing happened, no sound expect the monotonous clatter of the wheels under her knees. She opened her eyes, trying to accustom them to the dark, staring into it, dreading what she might see. Slowly the darkness began to lift, showing outlines, shapes. She focused her eyes on them.

They were people. Sitting on the floor in front of her. No. not people. Children! Sitting close together, facing her.

She could see more clearly now, as if someone had switched a light on. She took in her surroundings: the closed traincar, the children. So many of them – the car was full of children, with hardly any space left.

What children were these? How had they come here? Could they be children from her village? All her friends who had refused to wave to her, and others – from the school, from other villages? But no, she had never seen any of these before.

The children sat there, quietly rocking with the train and watching her: large wondering eyes fixed on her from all sides. She looked back, no longer afraid. Her shoulders slumped, and for a moment she felt nothing but fatigue and headache.

A girl detached herself from the group, worked her way over to Biba, smiled and held out a hand to her. The sleeve of her outstretched arm had a star loosely sewn to it. A yellow six-pointed star – just like Biba's, just like the painted one on the door of the train that had swallowed up Mama. Biba looked at the child beside her, at a second, a third, at all of them – they all had stars sewn to their sleeves, just like herself. She was glad of it: it made her feel that she had landed in the right place after all.

She dried her tears, took the girl's hand and together they crept closer to the other children. Now she could see them properly: they sat tightly packed together, and at first she thought that perhaps they were chained to one another. Then she realized that they were sitting like that for lack of room, that they had crowded too many children in just this one car.

She looked at their stars again, wondered why they all had them, whether they had all received them from that same young officer at the station. She thought it very likely, because all the stars were very precisely similar. In that case, maybe that officer hadn't been as nasty as he seemed? Maybe he had thought they were special: maybe he had chosen just these children out of all the children in the world, and given them stars so they would recognize each other. The thought pleased her. No doubt these children were smiling at her now on account of her star, were shifting a little to make room for her – accepting her because she had a star, too.

It wasn't easy to find a place for Biba. One girl showed her how to arrange her arms and legs, how to lay her head in one child's lap and lie down in such a way that her body would serve as a pillow for another child. Someone covered her bare feet with a sweater. When she closed her eyes she imagined that all the other children must have closed their eyes, too.

Now, no longer tense, her limbs relaxing, she suddenly felt how badly her head ached. The clatter of the train seemed to grow louder, to pound inside her head. She felt dizzy. Strange scenes with ugly, contorted faces in them appeared behind her closed eyes. She felt nauseated, tried to think of other things, of something happy, something quite remote from this car, these children.

It was very quiet now – no sound except the wheels of the train. The children didn't speak, didn't move, but Biba felt they weren't sleeping, were all staring into the darkness like herself now, each busy with his own thoughts, his own images of the people dear to him.

As if in response, a low whimper came from somewhere

in the car, a faint voice calling: "Mama!"

"Mama!" repeated Biba in a soft moan, as though uttering a prayer.

"Mama!" whispered the child in her lap.

Biba's heart swelled. She wanted to cry out, and she wanted to sink into sleep hugging this most wonderful of all words in her arms.

Three

The light was coming through a narrow crack in the wall of the car. It filtered through as a pale-coloured rainbow, and rose to the ceiling in the shape of a trembling, transparent streak. Hitting the ceiling, it shattered, and its splinters fell upon the dark lump on the floor, tracing the huddled children.

Biba was awake. She had not slept at all, had cried all night. It had been a long, difficult night, filled with terror and darkness and nausea. Now, with the first signs of day showing, Biba felt some relief, and with it a great fatigue. She felt that now she could sleep, but was too wide awake to attempt it.

She gazed straight in front of her. The ray of light played over her face, like the light from a mirror held by a teasing child. She blinked, but did not turn away, went on looking at the light, the radiant fragment of sun. It reminded her of the morning mist she had seen once, long ago.

It had still been dark when she had gone out with Ivica, and the village was still sunk in slumber, all empty except for the sheep that came bustling and bleating out of courtyards to join Ivica's herd. Then, trampling the tall dew-drenched grass, the sheep made their way down to the valley. Biba and Ivica ran alongside, each guarding one flank, driving them towards the path that led down to the large meadow and the teeming wood in the valley below. There were tall ferns to struggle with on the way, prickly bushes and nettles to avoid, a small copse of young trees to cross – a long way to go to the valley which kept receding with every step, and then was suddenly there, before them. The sheep recognized their valley and took the last stretch at a run. Freed from responsibility for the flock, which was safe here and could graze undisturbed, Biba and Ivica went on to the wood to pick blackberries, peeping through their foliage like dark purple drops. The spring morning was everywhere, fragrant in trees and soil, joyous in bird chatter. And they ran, chased rabbits, threw their arms round tree trunks, climbed up into the branches, hunted for mushrooms, acorns, or some great secret harboured by the dense forest; deep into it they went, wishing that something unusual would happen to them. At last they grew tired, sat, resting against a tree, eating berries and watching the sunrise. A broad bar of sundust broke trembling through the foliage, silvering dew on the budding boughs. It widened, became a rainbow straining to emerge from the clouds, spreading a silver carpet at the feet of the rising sun.

Just such a rainbow as that poured through the crack in the wall.

Biba looked about her.

She was lying with her head cradled in the lap of a child, who was in turn cradled by another, and that one by another again. They lay in a large heap of intertwined bodies, and they were all asleep.

The car resembled a stable, with only one small window high up by the ceiling. The wooden floor on which the children lay was filthy. A covered bucket stood in the only free corner, and it shook with the train's motion and gave out a foul smell.

Biba's eyes returned to the children, studying their faces one by one. They looked all alike to her: she could hardly distinguish between them, or retain an impression of any single face. Her glance fell on the sweater covering her feet, and she stared at it for a while, knowing only that it wasn't hers. She looked at the girl in whose lap she lay: somehow this face was different from the others, it had some connection with the sweater. Suddenly she remembered – remembered it all as though someone had whispered it into her ear. Now she knew where she was, how she had got here – knew she was on a train, a traincar, being taken to an unknown destination. She knew she was here alone, without Mama, with children as forlorn as herself, bearing stars on the sleeves like her own.

She did not feel sad. She felt nothing. She removed the sweater and spread it over the girl beside her.

Her eyes traveled round the car. A wooden wall ran to a corner, met another, shorter wall, which also ran to a corner and into another wall again. All the walls were made of rough wooden boards, and they all ran into corners, and all the corners together with the walls, like the floor the children lay on, was made of irregular boards, warped and pitted and dry.

If the car should turn upside down, they'd be all lying on the ceiling.

Maybe it would be nicer that way?

Her eyes went back to the crack in the wall, the one that had let in the sunbeam before. Slowly she moved, careful not to wake the others, wriggled over to the crack and looked out.

Low, sun-parched grass grew along the tracks. Beyond it, as far as the eye could see – nothing; no houses, hills, trees, people – nothing but dusty shrubs and yellowing grass.

It didn't surprise her. This was an entirely different sort of train from the one that had taken them from the village. That train had had soft springy seats, a mirror overhead on one wall and a pretty landscape picture on the other. There had been a small folding table-top under the window between the seats, and the window itself had been large and had even had a curtain. And past that window had swept green fields and forest and rivers, flocks of sheep, pretty houses with red roofs, people, children, shepherds...

To be sure, this also was a train: its wheels clattered monotonously, its engine whistled and belched smoke, but here there were only four rough wooden walls, four corners with a ceiling on top. Naturally, it would be different outside as well.

The children were waking up. One child stirring was enough to rouse all the rest. Soon they were all up – stretching, yawning, rubbing their eyes, many still half asleep, some crying. Presently they began to talk, and Biba realized with a dismay that they were speaking a medley of foreign languages and that she didn't understand a word they said. It soon struck her that many of them didn't understand each other. Quite a few spoke Grandma Language. The one word they all understood, however, was "Mama".

They were all dressed differently, too: in nighties, frocks, heavy overcoats, some wore shoes and others were barefoot, some wore caps, some carried schoolbags and were dressed in their school uniforms; some wore the yellow star on their sleeves, others on their chests. Biba had the impression that they had all been traveling together for a long time already. She could not say what it was about them that made her think so, but she felt quite certain of it.

A box was placed in the middle of the car, and a big girl sat down on it. The youngest children collected round her, and stood waiting for her to comb their hair, braid it, button up frocks, tie shoelaces. Some just came to show themselves to her and receive her assurance that they had dressed and combed themselves properly. One girl with long golden curls was holding a pair of red ribbons in her hand, trying to straighten them out, and puckering her lips as though on the point of tears. She pushed her way over to the Big Girl and asked shakily: "Where's my mummy?"

"But that's just where we are going – to see her!" the Big Girl said, adjusting her dress and combing the bright curls. The golden-haired girl had already forgotten her question: she laughed, babbled, and when the Big Girl was finished with her, willingly made way for the next child in turn.

In a while the children began to drift off, form into groups. In one corner, girls were playing "house". They had a ragdoll and a cardboard box, and they had decorated the box so beautifully that it looked fit for a queen. They dressed the doll, combed its hair, "bathed" it, and talked to it as if each of them was a mother and the doll her child. A bit further away, some boys were playing marbles; another group played jacks; another – cat's cradle.

Only the corner with the bucket was crowded. A girl was standing there, hugging the wall, unable to make up her mind whether she wanted to sit down on the bucket or not. She was looking about her as though begging for help. One boy with a peaked cap on his head gave a nod of understanding, and began to turn all the other boys away.

Even that didn't help, though. The girl continued standing by the wall, tears in her eyes, a look of anxiety on her face. The others stood and watched her, as though waiting along with her to see what would happen. One of them said:

"Go on! We'll hide you."

But the girl made no move. Very likely she just hadn't understood; none of them spoke her language.

Now the Big Girl came over, but she couldn't speak the girl's language either. She thought for a minute, and then an idea seemed to strike her. She motioned the children aside and began a swift, purposeful search of the car. Presently she found what she was looking for: an old shabby leather belt which had been lying on the floor all the time.

She returned to the bucket and began to look for nails in the walls on the other side of it. She found just what she needed on one side, and on the other she pulled a nail out of the wall and hammered it into place with her shoe, at some height above the bucket and right opposite the other nail. She hooked the belt to one nail, circled the bucket and hooked the other end to the second nail. Then she turned to the children, who had been following her every move with eager curiosity. She opened her mouth to say something, remembered that not all of them would understand, and resolved to show them what she wanted. She pulled her sweater off over her head, unhooked one end of the belt, passed it through both sleeves, hooked the belt to its nail again – and the sweater hung there like a piece of curtain. She turned to the others, went through a little mime of undressing, and pointed at them.

The children exchanged glances, then went into action – removing coats, sweaters, jackets, and handing them to the Big Girl. She passed the belt through all the sleeves, hooked it back into place on the two nails, and lo – a splendid patchwork curtain was hiding the bucket from view!

All the children came over to admire the curtain, clapping their hands, exclaiming. The girl who had been the occasion for it all smiled happily. The Boy in the Peaked Cap approached her, lifted a corner of the curtain, and with a broad sweep of his hand invited her in:

"Please, my lady!"

The girl laughed, went behind the curtain.

They couldn't get enough of it: it was like playing "Theatre". Now they all wanted to go there, and the Big Girl had to keep order: a child would go in at one side, and come out at the other. All who came out were smiling as though they had seen some wondrous sight behind the curtain.

Eventually the game's novelty wore off. The bucket stank, and its evil smell spread through the car. In a while they went back to their corners, their games.

The golden-haired girl began crying again, asking over and over: "Where's my mummy?", "Where's my mummy?'', the Big Girl repeating wearily: "We're going to her, we're going to her.''

Now a little boy started crying, too. A few others joined in, then still others, their wails growing louder and louder. The Big Girl tried to comfort them, but as that failed she gathered the youngest of them round her box and began telling them stories.

She spoke in a sort of gentle singsong voice, but loud enough for the others to hear her as well. Gradually they stopped what they were doing and listened - at first from their places, then crawling over to the box one by one and settling down there. Many children did not understand her, but they caught the drift of her story from her gestures and mimicry, and from the songs she sang from time to time. The small children calmed down, some fell asleep, the others listened quietly.

"...And at last the day of the prince's ball arrived. Cinderella's stepmother and her two stepsisters drove to the palace in a grand carriage, and only Cinderella stayed at home. Her stepmother had left her a huge bag of beans to be sorted, and had told her to mind and finish it all by the time they returned. Cinderella sat down to work right away, but she was feeling very, very sad about having to miss the ball. She was sure that if only her mother had still been alive, she would certainly have let her go, too.

"Suddenly she heard a voice saying: 'Don't be sad, Cinderella, I have come to help you.'

"Cinderella looked – and there stood a lovely fairy with a magic wand in her hand.

"'You wish you were going to the prince's ball too, don't you?' said the fairy.

"'Oh, I do!' whispered Cinderella, hardly believing her eyes.

"'Well,' said the fairy, 'if you wish to go – you shall' – and she touched Cinderella with her magic wand. A cloud of dust rose up about her, and when the dust sank – there stood Cinderella in the most beautiful golden dress you ever saw – a dress fit for a princess. Never in her life had Cinderella seen such a pretty dress, nor such pretty slippers with real high heels – so high she could hardly walk in them. She went to the well to look at her reflection in the water, and the sight nearly took her breath away. Then the fairy took her by the hand and led her back to the house, and there Cinderella saw six little mice skipping about a huge pumpkin. The fairy touched the mice and the pumpkin, and again there rose a cloud of dust, and out of it appeared a magnificent golden carriage harnessed to six of the whitest horses that ever were. Then the fairy turned to Cinderella and said:

"'Go to the ball, and have a good time, but remember: you must be home before midnight, for on the stroke of midnight my magic wears off...'"

The children had forgotten where they were. The Big Girl's clear singsong voice had transported them to another world, an enchanted world of princes and princesses, fairies and magic spells. The clatter of the train wheels had become the carriage driving Cinderella to the ball; the train whistle was a golden clock chiming the midnight hour; the smoke from the engine was the dust raised by the galloping horses taking Cinderella home in her carriage.

The air in the car had grown oppressive. The ceiling and the walls gave off heat, the sun shone full through the small window, and the stench from the bucket was overpowering. But the children noticed none of it – they were following Cinderella's fortunes, worried lest she fail to return in time.

The Big Girl was about to begin a new story when the train braked suddenly and pulled to a stop.

They heard steps outside, voices, people talking. The steps drew near, the door opened slowly, a soldier boarded the train. He did not look at them but remained in the doorway, his eyes searching for something. Then he saw the curtain. He cast a furious glance at the children, and his face seemed to say: "Who did this? Just you wait!"

Swiftly he strode over to the curtain, tore it down, and removed the bucket with a look of disgust on his face. The children sat close together, motionless, waiting. The soldier came back, restored the bucket, empty and clean. Someone outside handed him a basket of bread and a jug of water, which he dumped on the floor. Then he left and the train set out again.

And still the children did not move, sat with their eyes fixed on the door through which the soldier had left. He came every day, always going through the same motions: removing the bucket, returning it empty, shoving bread and water at them, and leaving. And every day the children would sit and stare at the door long after he had left, not speaking, keeping their thoughts to themselves. But in his heart each of them hoped that today something would happen, that the door would open and instead of a soldier it would be Mama there. Or that it would open to let them out, breathe the fresh air, see the light, the day, the sky. That it would open and *not* let the soldier in...

But it was always the soldier, and he never said anything, did anything, touched anyone. He did not even have a rifle, just bread and water, but he always left an air of despondency behind – and with it the first seeds of hatred.

As though falling in with their mood, the Big Girl resumed her storytelling in a low voice, almost in a whisper: it was the story of the terrible man-eating giant and of his seven-league boots with which he could leap over hill and dale, lake and forest.

"And when the giant came home he found the seven dwarves waiting for him. They had lost their way in the forest, and they begged him to let them stay the night, not knowing what a wicked giant he was. 'Oh goodie,' thought the giant, 'they will make a lovely breakfast tomorrow morning' –and he welcomed them in the beds of his seven daughters, who were just as wicked as himself.

"Luckily, though the dwarves heard him talking to his daughters, and so they learnt of the terrible fate in store for them.

"How could they save themselves? They thought and thought they talked and argued, and then all at once the youngest dwarf said:

" 'I know! Let's switch nightcaps with his daughters, and when he comes in the morning and sees our nightcaps, he will think it's us, and he will eat up his daughters in our stead.' "

Slowly the story took grip on them. Their minds still bore the soldier's image as he had stood there scowling, hatless, angry; but another image was taking shape beside it: the image of the man-eating giant. And as the story went on,

56

the two images fused and soldier and giant became one.

"And that is what they did," the Big Girl continued. "And when the giant came into the bedroom the next morning, he was so hungry that he didn't think much: he just turned to where he saw the dwarves' nightcaps peeping out from under the blanket, grabbed them without looking and swallowed them one by one. Meanwhile the dwarves themselves had slipped out of the room. They took the seven-league boots, crept into them, and leaped over hill and dale and arrived home safe and sound."

Relieved, the children jumped up and began dancing round the Big Girl, feet stamping in rhythm, hands banging on the walls of the car. Gradually, still dancing, they drew near the door, pounded on it with all their might, fists clenched as though to strike the soldier when he should appear.

The Boy in the Peaked Cap turned to the corner with the bucket, stood there like a knight in armour facing a terrible dragon, his loyal band of followers behind him. He looked at the children as though asking for their support, and they stopped beating on the door, watching him expectantly. He bent, picked up the torn curtain, straightened it out, and with a resolute gesture fixed it back into place. Then he stood back triumphantly and declared:

"The curtain shall stay here forever, and we shall let no one remove it!"

"Hurray! Hurray!" shouted the children, and broke into a dance again.

The Big Girl tapped the waterjug. At first they thought she was drumming out a rhythm to their dance, but when she tapped harder and called out to them, they turned to her questioningly, hushing one another to catch her cry of: "Breakfast! Breakfast!"

They began to gather round her box – slowly, reluctant to leave their game. Gradually they calmed down, found places as if by a fixed seating arrangement. The Big Girl shared out the bread, the Boy in the Peaked Cap helping her.

She had some chocolate sprinkles left, but as there wasn't enough to go round, the Big Girl suggested letting only the very youngest children have it, and they all agreed.

Biba had stayed by her crack in the wall all this time. Now, watching the children eat, she felt a sudden urge to hide, to escape, get out of here. She was seized by an obscure panic. Was it because of the soldier, because of the scary giant story she had never heard before, or because of something unknown and indefinable? She felt lonely too. No one had even noticed her staying apart, her failure to join in their games. She was just thinking of that when the Boy in the Peaked Cap came over, crouched before her, held out a piece of bread, smiled at her and said in her own language:

"Eat it slowly, in tiny crumbs. Eat it the way birds do, so you won't be hungry again too soon, because you'll get nothing else before tomorrow."

She thanked him and did as he told her. He waited to make sure she had understood, then with a satisfied nod, turned away. Her eyes followed him, and her heart filled with relief and gratitude to know that at least one other child spoke her language. And not just any child, but *he*, the

Head Boy, the bravest of them all. She felt he was precious to her, like a close relative.

The day passed, and what light had come in through the small window under the ceiling faded. Inside the car it grew dark, as though someone had lowered the blinds.

The children were settling down for the night, finding a corner, a wall for support, a lap to rest their heads in. Biba had waited a long time for this moment. All day she had made plans for going to the corner behind the curtain, and now at last, with the car in darkness and everyone lying down, she felt her way carefully along the wall to the bucket. Even the thought of being *heard* to go there embarrassed her, and she gave a sigh of relief when it was all over.

Now she had nowhere to lie down. All the good places were already taken, even the one by the crack in the wall – all except the corner near the bucket, where the stench was too heavy. She was still searching for a place when the Boy in the Peaked Cap noticed her.

"Hey, you," he called softly. "Come here!"

She crawled over to where he lay on a piece of sacking, and he shifted a little to make room for her. She thanked him in a whisper and lay down – but stiffly, her body too tense to compose itself for sleep.

She did not want to sleep anyhow: she wanted to talk. There were so many things she had to ask him. He would be sure to know everything – so brave as he had been today when he repaired the curtain. How to begin, though? What to say to him? And maybe he was already asleep? Or didn't feel like talking? Or was tired?

She lay still, listening, heard the monotonous clatter of

the wheels and the rattle of the bucket in the corner, but those were noises they had all grown used to – no doubt they would wake up if they stopped.

All at once he whispered in her ear: "Are you asleep?"

"No."

"Me neither. Want to talk?"

"Mm."

They sat up, careful not to disturb the others, remained silent.

At last he spoke up.

"What's your name?"

"Biba. And yours?"

"Vlado."

Another brief silence, and then he asked:

"Are you at school already?"

"Not yet. Next year."

"Me, I'm in Third Grade."

"Really?" she said, awed.

They fell silent again. Now Biba made bold to ask:

"Listen, where are we going?"

"Far away. To another country."

"What's the country called?"

"Camp."

"You ever been there?"

"No." His manner told Biba that he did not care to pursue the subject. Now he was lowering himself as well, lying down on his back.

Alarmed by this sign that the conversation was over, that he meant to go to sleep, Biba asked quickly:

"How long have you been on the train?"

"Three days."

"And the others?"

"Oh, much longer. They were already here when I came. Only you yourself came later than me. Some of them have been on this train ages."

"You know, I don't understand what they're saying at all – most of them. They talk so funny."

"That's because they're all from different countries, so they speak different languages, you see?"

"Mm."

The one question Biba had wanted to ask from the outset was if he knew where all the mothers were, but the mere thought of Mama put a lump in her throat. She was afraid of bursting into tears if she just said the word "Mama", and then Vlado would think she was just a cry-baby. She resolved not to ask him about it – but there were other questions.

"Vlado?" – she felt a bit shy, calling him by his name like that.

"What?"

"Why do we all have stars?"

"Because we are Jews," he said, as if that explained it all.

"What's 'Jews'?"

"I don't know."

Another silence. Then Vlado said, "Let's go to sleep now," and arranged himself on the sacking.

"All right," said Biba, but when she lay down, his hair brushing against her cheek, she took courage and asked quickly, trying to sound casual:

"And the mothers? Where are they?"

"I don't know." He spoke softly, thoughtfully, as if the question had bothered him as well, as if he had been ready for it, waiting for her to ask him from the start. "I think that perhaps they're on this train, too. I saw them take my mother to a car that looked just the same as this one."

"My mother too," whispered Biba, straining to choke her tears back.

They lay still now, not speaking, but wide awake.

What if it were true what Vlado said? What if Mama were here on this train? Agitated, she drew a deep breath, began to consider her surroundings from this new angle. Really, how come it hadn't struck her before? How come she hadn't remembered that the car which had swallowed Mama had looked exactly like this one? And that its wooden door had a star painted on it just like the star on their sleeves, only much bigger. Maybe even right next to their own. Maybe she too, was lying on the floor like Biba here, by the wall. Maybe even by the same wall, only on the other side, but with the same wheels turning under her. Maybe the soldier brought her bread in the morning. Maybe she could even see her...

The desire to see Mama came over her with such fearful urgency that she shot bolt upright. Oh, she would get to her feet, step over Vlado, flatten herself against the wall and call out to her: "Mama!" No, no not the wall – the door! The door that always let only the soldier in, that was always locked. She would pull at it with her might, open it, jump down, run to the next car, open its door, open all the doors of the cars one by one, pass the whole train and open its doors till she found Mama.

She felt a vast strength in herself, the strength to accomplish all this. In a moment it became so overpowering that she could not stay still, had to act on it. She rose to her knees in the darkness, stared at the sleeping children, at the door trembling on its hinges: how big it was, much bigger than usual, much bigger than by day, and closed by a thousand locks.

Her eyes returned to the wall. She crept nearer, touched it, pressed her face against it, her lips. She shut her eyes and pictured Mama on the other side. Maybe she, too, had pressed her face against the wall, maybe at just the same spot, maybe there was nothing but a thin wooden partition between them. Mama was there – she *had* to be.

Biba laid her tear-stained cheek against the wall and softly cried out to her – "Mama!"

Four

When Biba awoke next morning , all the others were already up. The small children were combed and tidy, the queue by the curtain had dwindled to a trickle; most of the children had already formed into groups, resumed the games they had started yesterday. One of the largest groups had collected around Vlado and were playing "school". Vlado himself, as the oldest, was naturally the teacher. He had made everyone sit into two straight rows, their hands crossed behind them as in a proper classroom. Now he called one girl to the "blackboard". She stood, came over, hands still on back, looked up at him. Vlado was holding up three fingers, and you could tell from the girl's frowning concentration that she was thinking hard.

"Come on! How many fingers? Count them!"

"Three," said the girl, counting them with her chin, her hands being occupied gripping one another on her back.

"And here?" – holding his other hand up.

"Uh..." this time it took longer. "Five," she said at last, rather uncertainly.

"Now," said Vlado, "if you add up these three fingers here, and there five here, how many will there be altogether?"

This proved too much for her. Two or three children whispered the answer at her, and when Vlado caught them at it he was so cross that he put them in the corner. Then he gave the girl a bad mark, and told another girl off for giggling.

Now he noticed Biba and invited her to join them, but Biba shook her head. She didn't care for such a silly game. She herself could already count up to a thousand, she could read, and add up without the aid of her fingers. She knew that three and five were eight with hardly to have to think about it. Besides, she wanted to take up the place by the crack before some other child appropriated it.

She went and looked out. This time she hardly glanced at the passing countryside, which still remained barren and yellow and lifeless. This time she studied the train, their train. What was behind their own car? Were there any more cars at all? And if so – what did they look like? Was the engine near or far? She would have to wait for a curve in the tracks: She could see nothing so long as the train went straight.

Presently it turned, and she saw the other cars: there were a great many of them, all resembling her own. They were all closed and windowless, and looked like enormous wooden crates with only one small opening just below the roof. The engine was quite near – only a single car separated it from her own.

She studied the other cars. What was inside them? Sacks? Animals? She had seen just such cars being loaded with cows and sheep. But perhaps these carried neither cows nor sheep nor sacks – but children? Big and small children with stars, children who wept like the golden-haired girl and kept asking: "Where's my mummy?" Children who cried in chorus: "Ma-ma!" It was funny, come to think of it, how all children, whatever their language, called their mother "mama". Or at least something very like it – always *sounding* like "mama" anyway. Yet perhaps it wasn't *all* who called their mother something like "mama", but only children with stars?

The cars were traveling in a straight line behind her own again. She could see nothing anymore, but kept her eye resolutely to the crack, waiting for the next curve to inspect the cars more closely. She listened to the clatter of the wheels, and it seemed to change as she listened, to be saying something – to repeat what Vlado had told her yesterday: "Perhaps they're on this train, too. I saw them take my mother to a car that looked just the same as this."

A great pent-up sigh shook her frame: "Mama! Mami!"

But maybe it wasn't just *her* Mama. It was every child's mama. Maybe all the mothers were there, all together in one car?

Yes, the mother of every child here must be right there in the next car, and the children don't even know it. But they ought to be told! She must tell them. She must tell them – and then all the children will get up as one, stand by the crack and shout: "Ma-ma!" And the mothers will hear, they are bound to hear. If they all shout together they will overcome the noise of wheels and engine. Maybe it will help if they pound their fists on the wall, stamp on the floor, make so much noise that the mothers hear them. How can they sit there so calmly, play games, listen to stories, sleep –

while right here beside them, almost within hand's reach, are their mamas. How come they don't know it? She must tell them.

She was just about to turn, speak to them, when she felt the train start on another bend. She glued her eye to the crack: if only she could pierce those wooden boards with her glance! Peep inside and make certain that Mama was really there.

What are they doing there, the mothers? Very likely they sit on the floor together, combing their hair, helping each other do up buttons and hooks and ribbons, telling stories, playing games. Oh, rubbish! Who ever saw mothers act like that?

But then what? What are they doing?

Surely they don't just sit there quietly like the children. No doubt they prowl round the car, scurry about, beat on the walls, search for some opening, try to scratch out some hole, beat on the door, climb to the window, shout, scream, try to force the door. And when they find it is all in vain – they weep, tear their hair out, beat their heads against the wall, call their children's names. And when that doesn't help either, when no one comes to open the door, answer their cries – then each of them sits in a corner apart, or squats by a crack in the wall. Each mother knows only one thing: that her child is there, in that other car, and she can't get to him. And when the soldier comes with the bread and water they set upon him, seek to trample him, break out, escape, and he must summon more soldiers to his aid because the mothers are too much for him. The soldiers come and force them back into the car, striking them with their rifle butts, perhaps even stabbing them with their bayonets. But the mothers feel nothing. They hit out wildly, pushing and crying: "Give me my child!"

Each mother cries out in her own language: "Give me my child! My child!"

Yes, that's it, definitely: all the mothers cry and call out, just like her own mama. Maybe even now, right this minute, they stand there pounding on the rough wooden boards, calling their names. And the children hear nothing. She ought to tell them. They ought to get up and shout and shout till they are heard over the noise of the wheels and the engine, shout till the mothers hear them.

She must talk to them, tell them.

But how? They don't know her language.

The Big Girl tapped the waterjug, called the children to breakfast. Only then Biba realized how late she had slept, how the bread-and-water soldier had already been and gone.

She would have liked to stay by her crack like yesterday, but Vlado beckoned to her, and when she shook her head he came and pulled her into the ring round the box, made room for her beside him. She wanted to tell him about the other cars, and about the mothers being there, but was afraid it would sound silly. All at once it didn't seem real anymore, even to herself. Besides, Vlado knew everything, and no doubt he knew better than her if the mothers were there or not, and it wasn't for her to tell him.

Each child received his slice of bread, but there were no more chocolate sprinkles today. The bread was dry and stale, and the small children refused to eat it. Some were already beginning to cry, but before their crying could spread to the others, the Big Girl picked up the empty chocolate tin, and started going round from one child to the next, pretending to share out the chocolate. She would put her hand into the tin, make a sprinkling movement with her fingers over each slice of bread, then smile and say:

"Here's some chocolate for you," or "Is that sweet enough?" or "Mm, good isn't it?"

The big children knew there wasn't any chocolate there, but they helped the Big Girl pretend – turning to the little ones beside them, asking if the sprinkles were sweet, if tasty, making believe they were longing to have some, too, pretending to envy the little ones, licking their lips – and everyone was happy. The small children were virtually convinced they were eating chocolate, and the big ones were happy for having convinced them.

In the middle of the make-believe meal, the train pulled abruptly to stop. The wheels screeched, the children fell against each other, the bucket slithered from its corner to the centre of the car, the Big Girl and Vlado grabbed the jug to keep the water from spilling, and the train stood.

They were puzzled, looked at each other, then turned expectantly to the door.

They heard steps, a hubbub of voices, people running. One voice, louder than the rest, called out an order. The car began to move again, but slowly, as if pushed from behind and not pulled by the engine, the wheels soundless expect for an occasional click. They sat staring at the door, hushed, waiting. They knew something was about to happen, something out of the ordinary.

Some children made a ladder of hands and shoulders for Vlado, and he climbed to the window, looked out, and announced that all the other cars were gone, that there was just one roofless car filled with soldiers behind them, and the engine in front. Worried, the children sought cracks in the wall to see for themselves.

The train stopped, then moved on with a hoarse grating of wheels, like a person clearing his throat before starting to sing.

"Come here!" the Big Girl called, as though seeking to draw their attention away from what was happening outside. "We haven't drunk our water yet."

They went and lined up for their half cups of water. They had gone through the same procedure every day, but today it was different; today it seemed to have a special significance. One by one they approached the jug, drank their ration and handed the cup to the next in line. Then they all sat down with their eyes on the door, ears straining to catch the sound of the wheels, trying to interpret it, trying to understand why they were moving so slowly.

The train creaked to a stop once more. It had stopped many times before on this journey, but they had always known it would move again. Now it just stood there. Why? And where was the soldier? Why didn't he come? What were these sounds? It seemed as though there were a lot of people outside, and as if more were coming all the time.

They waited, tense, watchful. Then the door opened and three soldiers bounded up the steps. Someone outside slid the other half of the door open as well, and the full sunlight struck their eyes – blinding them, making them turn away, clap their hands over their faces. The soldier approached, and sensing their nearness the children peered through their fingers, spread them a little, tried to accustom their eyes bit by bit to the dazzling sunlight.

Then, as the children just sat, their soldier came and pointed at them and at the door: they were to come out.

The Big Girl stood, still shading her eyes with one hand, turned to the others and said in a calm soothing voice:

"Get up, we are there!"

They scrambled to their feet, shading their eyes as she did, crowding round her.

"Each of the big children will look after a small one," she said, speaking up to make herself heard over the cries and whimpered protests of the youngest. "We'll have to carry them because they can't get down by themselves. The steps are very high and narrow and dangerous, and you are to be careful. All right, everybody – the door is open: we can leave."

She took the golden-haired girl who asked "Where's my mummy?" on one arm, then picked up her own little sister, Esty. Holding them both close against her, she turned to the exit, glancing back to see whether the others had understood and were following her example. Briefly they watched her, then Vlado took Biba and the shy girl of the bucket, led them to the door and lifted them down, the soldiers lending a hand.

Outside, the light still hurting their eyes, they reeled like drunkards and had to sit down at once. They felt as if the earth were moving under them, as if they themselves were still moving, the wheels still rattling and the floor rocking under their feet.

It took a long time for the smells of grass, soil, stone and fresh air to reach their senses, a long time before they grasped these things were real – not a memory or an illusion, but here all round them. Slowly, their eyes still shut, they touched the ground, patted it, began to explore their surroundings with probing hands. Little by little, they adjusted themselves to the out-of-doors – to the light, the day, the space around them, the sky overhead. One after the other they opened their eyes, sniffed the air, stared at the grass, and realized they were no longer shut up in a dark and stuffy car – that they had solid ground under them, no longer a swaying void, unseen but guessed at – that they were out in the open again.

Seeing that the children had recovered from their first meeting with the broad daylight, the soldiers ordered them up. One by one, supporting each other, still a bit unsteady on their feet, but no longer protesting, they rose, formed a line, and were counted. Then some soldiers left, and some others took charge of the children and began to lead them down the railway embankment to the field below. The children walked in pairs, guarded by two soldiers in front, two behind, and two on each side, with a fairly great distance between them.

The train sounds of engine and wheels, whistle and clatter, still rang in their ears, but every step they took increased their confidence. Some of the children could not keep up with the pace and fell behind, breaking the ranks, but the soldiers were patient, waiting for them to catch up again and move on. At every turning in the path the soldiers stopped to count them, making sure no one had escaped.

Their road narrowed to a pass between high rocks, and when it emerged again they paused, lost in wonder at the view of the vast green valley opening before them. It was there that the soldiers were taking them.

Walking became more difficult. They were going downhill now, but there was no longer any sign of path or track, and they moved gingerly – helping each other over puddles, rocks nettles, pushing on through the tall scratchy growth, putting lizards and grasshoppers to flight. They kept stumbling, bumping into each other and into the soldiers. It was worst for the shoeless children, who scratched their bare feet on thorns, cut them on stones, and shrank for fear of stepping on a worm, a lizard or a cricket.

Willy-nilly, the soldiers abandoned the effort to keep them in line. Instead of shoving them back with their rifle butts each time, they just strolled casually beside them. Whenever they judged that the group had become too widely scattered, they stopped those in front, waited for the stragglers to catch up, counted them, and went on.

At last they reached the valley they had seen from above, and it was even lovelier than they had imagined – a place of grass and flowers.

They felt released, as if the sense of being outside, in the air and the sun, had only now really penetrated; as if at last the earth had really stopped rocking under their feet, their bodies no longer throbbed with the wheels' clatter. Only now they grasped that they were really and truly free. Their faces lit up, grew cheerful, and soon the last traces of fright, confusion and uncertainty were gone. Now nothing existed but sky and clouds and birds and flowers, air and light, and infinite space. They knew at last that this was what they had missed in the stifling traincar.

A light breeze blew, cooling their faces, bringing life and joy. Suddenly they began to speak, chatter to each other in every language. They laughed, pulled the girls' braids, flung their arms at the sky as though to pluck the clouds, chased lizards, hunted beetles. The soldiers walked alongside but did not restrain them, nor were the children troubled by their presence: they had come to take them for granted as the stars on their sleeves, as something that was just always *there*. The soldiers did not order them about, did not push them back into line, did not rebuke them. Even their walk had changed from the jackbooted tramp of before to an easy saunter, matching the children's pace. They walked in twos or threes, talking together. Some had even removed their belts, unbuttoned tunics, thrust caps into pockets, lighted cigarettes. They stretched themselves, breathed the fresh air.

Happy, carefree, the children moved about the meadow as if they knew no other, as if this meadow were their home, their familiar playground. The soldiers watched, and presently they joined the children – picking a flower here and there, looking for clover leaves, chasing butterflies, whistling on grass-blades. And it seemed as though the children, too, forgot that these were soldiers – the same soldiers who had shouted at them, flung them into the train and kept them locked in their foul-smelling car. Here, in this lovely valley, it was all forgotten, and the soldiers were like older boys in school uniforms – bare-headed, breath-less, their rifles dangling loosely on their backs – older boys who had been given weapons and told to play "soldiers".

Like the Big Girl, like Vlado, the soldiers looked after the youngest children, helping them over obstacles, carrying them in their arms when they grew tired, extracting a thorn from one boy's foot. Vlado caught a hedgehog and they all gathered round, touching its spines with wary fingers, teasing it, till one of the soldiers said they ought to release it, put it under a rock or it would die, and they pitied the hedgehog and did as the soldier said.

Slowly they crossed the valley, children and soldiers, as if they neither knew nor cared where they were going.

The sun stood high in the sky and the day had grown hot by the time they reached a cluster of wooden huts, which you could hardly even call a "place". The huts looked deserted, half burnt down, without roofs or windows, here and there only a bare concrete floor showing where a hut had once stood. The site was marked off by a barbed-wire fence, and it, too, was torn down in spots.

The soldiers halted, buttoned up their tunics, buckled their belts, retrieved caps, adjusted rifles – and the children concluded that they, too, must come to order. On their own, without being told, they gave hands, formed into pairs, and when the soldiers turned to give them the order they saw that the children were already standing in two neat lines, and were grinning mischievously as though to say: "Well? Fooled you, didn't we?"

The soldiers were marching again like proper soldiers with their rifles straight on their backs, and the children followed. They came to a halt before the only hut with a roof and were told to wait.

Now they had time to look about. The ground here was barren, without flowers or grass, dirty and littered with empty tins, broken cases, children's shoes, yellowing cartons and rusty iron. The place looked like an old garbage dump or an abandoned settlement. The soldiers told them to enter the hut, and they obeyed. The soldiers remained outside, and for a moment they lingered, soldiers and children regarding each other. Then the door closed and was bolted on the outside.

The children stayed where they were, listening, hearing the soldiers' steps slowly retreat, die away. All of a sudden there was nothing but a great silence, inside the hut and out. The children stared at the door and wondered why they had been shut up here and why the soldiers had left them; and the longer they stared at it the more it seemed as though the door would never open again. They could still feel the cool breeze of the valley on their flushed cheeks, the wind blowing through hair that now stuck damply to their sweating brows. For a while they remained still, then grew restless, shuffled their feet, looked at each other, demanded explanations from the bigger children. The place grew sultry. It grew hotter by the moment, as though they were inside a boiling cauldron and someone was fanning the flames underneath. They began to fidget, to move, to wander aimlessly about.

The heat was becoming unbearable. It simmered at them from the walls, from the roof that emitted tiny crackling sounds, from the window where the sun seemed to have got stuck. They swallowed, licked dry lips, wandered about in search of some slightly cooler spot. The flowers in their hands, faded, seemed to wither all at once as though touched by a deadly finger. The floor of the hut was too filthy to sit on. The looked at the door, strained their ears for some sound, but heard nothing except their own cries. Everyone had gone away, everyone had deserted them. They were alone. The silence outside filled them with anxiety. If only the soldiers had stayed with them!

Now, thirst came to aggravate heat and fear, and presently it became overwhelming. They began to prowl the hut, search the floor, rummage through the litter in hope to find a drop of water. Imprisoned within four sweltering walls, beneath a scorching roof, by a window with the sun stuck in it, they drifted about like sleepwalkers – parched, breathless, mumbling words that meant only one thing: "Water."

Even the Big Girl sought water.

At first she, too, had kept her eyes fixed on the door. Then she had tried to calm the children around her, promised them they would get water soon, but her voice lacked its old confidence. She seemed distracted, her eyes searching restlessly as she talked, making them feel helpless.

The children grew desperate. They tried to climb the walls, to find a crack, an opening, a way out. They beat on the door, besieged the Big Girl. They were suffocating, gasping for air, devoured by thirst. They knew the others were thirsty, too, and yet each knew only *his* thirst, *his* aching need for water.

The Big Girl made an effort: she collected the smallest children about her as she had on the train, began telling them a story, tried making them laugh at the doings of a handkerchief puppet, but no story or joke could take their minds off their consuming thirst. No one listened to her; only one word had meaning for them now: water.

"Water" they cried, "Water!"

A girl in a sleeveless dress, with the star tied around her bare arm, was crawling about the filthy floor. She was sniffing like a puppy, inspecting every object, stopping beside each child to hold up an empty cup and plead; "*Bitte – Wasser!*"

A boy snatched the cup from her hand under the illusion that the girl was *offering* them water. But the girl just retrieved her cup, continued on her round, begging from each child, groping about on the floor. She paused by a wad of paper, slowly began to pry it apart, as though seeking for a treasure inside. Whenever she managed to get a piece of paper loose, she threw it away without looking, as though not interested, as though picking at the paper out of sheer boredom. At last she gave up, went back to her painful crawling, her breath coming in harsh gasps. Suddenly she stopped in front of Biba, a look of amazement on her face.

During all this time, Biba had sat still in a corner. She was suffering, too of course, but she hadn't beaten on the door, shrieked, rushed wildly about, picked at papers. She sat, apparently unaware of the tears running down her face – and it was just those tears that had drawn the attention of the Girl with the Cup. Before Biba could move, escape the fascinated stare of those wide naked eyes, the girl pressed herself against Biba, seized Biba's head between both her hands, knelt, and with burning tongue began licking the tears from Biba's face.

Biba was terrified by those eyes, the face squeezed up

against her own. She wanted to run, hide, cry for help.

At that instant a voice called: "Soldiers!"

The Girl with the Cup gave a start, sprang back as though caught in a misdeed. Trembling, she threw herself on the floor, buried her face in her hands. Biba looked at her in dismay, uncertain whether she should get away from her as fast as possible or help her to her feet. The door opened and the children flung themselves at it. Biba, too, started for the door, then hesitated, moved back to the Girl with the Cup who lay sobbing on the floor. Biba shook her by the shoulder.

"Get up!" she cried. "Get up! The soldiers have come. They have opened the door. They are going to let us out, give us water. Do you hear? Water!"

The girl made no move. She dug her nails into the floor and wept. It flashed on Biba that the girl might not have understood, that very likely she spoke another language. She pulled the girl to her feet, began dragging her to the door, but when they were nearly there, the Girl with the Cup sank to the floor again, her body racked with sobs.

Biba looked for help, but all the other children were by the door, and many had already gone through. The soldier, though, was apparently making a selection among them – letting only the big children out and keeping the small ones back. Biba made a last attempt to raise the Girl with the Cup, but the soldier moved, seemed about to close the door. Biba jumped up.

"Wait!" she shouted in a panic, "Wait!" – and rushed at the door. Then she was outside and the door shut behind her.

The little children and the Girl with the Cup remained inside.

It was good to be out in the open again and to see soldiers about.

They lined up – boys to one side, girls to the other. It was hot outside, the sun blazing, the sand burning under their feet, but they stood – quiet, expectant, waiting.

But why had the little children been left behind in the hut? Because it was so hot here, perhaps, and they were better off inside after all? At least they were in the shade there. The hut was stuffy, to be sure, but it provided shelter from this fierce sun. If only they would give them some water to stop them crying so. The Girl with the Cup no doubt lay on the floor still crying too.

If only they'd give them water – to all of them!

Why were the soldiers standing in line as well? Why, when no one but the children were watching them! And why didn't they give them water? Why had they been made to stand like that facing each other? Well, someone had obviously given them an order to do so. Yes, and not given an order to fetch water. And soldiers couldn't just go and fetch water like that, could they? Someone had to tell them to. They were thirsty themselves: you just had to look at their dry lips to know. But they weren't allowed to drink either so long as no one had given the order.

Yes, they, too, had to wait, just like the children.

The sound of a motor engine came, drew near, stopped with a squeal of brakes behind the hut with the little children in it. Two soldiers appeared and right behind them – he: the Soldier with the Gold Buttons.

For a brief moment heat and thirst were forgotten: children and soldiers gazed wide-eyes at the approaching figure.

The soldiers drew themselves up, raised their chins, brought their heels together, gripped their rifles and stared dead ahead.

The children looked, enchanted by the gold cord sewn to his uniform, the white gloves, the shiny jackboots, the cap with its gold braid. For a while he just stood between the two rows of soldiers and children.

He was tall and fair. His uniform was brand-new, and everything about him was spotlessly clean, sleek and glossy. Every piece of braid, each golden button, shone bright; and brightest of all shone his tall black boots.

He moved swiftly past the long line of soldiers, and only stopped to issue a command to very last man in line. His speech was curt and compelling. The soldier clicked his heels and left at a run. The officer watched briefly to make sure his order was being carried out, then turned to the children.

At first he just looked at them all from a little distance, then crossed to the row of girls, stopping before the youngest at the end of the line – before Biba. He looked at her with a friendly expression on his face, as though he knew her, as though he had seen her somewhere and was trying to place her. Biba was completely dazzled by him – so marvellously handsome, so splendid as he was, like a proper fairy-tale prince. She could hardly believe he was smiling at her – at her of all the children, and with so many soldiers watching too. But he was – the corners of his mouth were definitely curled up.

Raising his stick, he adjusted the star on her sleeve a little. He did it so lightly, so delicately, that it felt like a caress, and Biba almost said thank-you. Still beaming, he cocked his head slightly as if about to whisper something in her ear, then moved on – turning once to send her a last smile and a wave of his stick. Biba took it as a greeting, since he obviously used the stick for a hand.

He inspected each child separately, lingering briefly before the shy girl who hadn't wanted to use the bucket, and before another with long plaits. He grinned at them all politely, as though welcoming them, but never stopped as long as he had before Biba. When he came to the end of the line, though, he suddenly paused in surprise.

Everyone, children and soldiers, looked to see what had surprised him so. It was the Big Girl.

The Soldier with the Golden Buttons folded his arms and surveyed her with evident satisfaction, as though he had finally found what he had been looking for all the time. She stood at the head of the line, being the tallest, taller even than the biggest of the boys. At first she looked back at him – this elegant man who showed such an interest in her – but she soon grew confused and lowered her eyes.

He stepped back, studying her from some distance the way one studies a picture, then returned and lifted her long hair with his stick, contemplating the effect. As the Big Girl still kept her eyes on the ground, he raised her chin with his stick, and she was forced to hold her head up but still refused to look at him. He persisted, though – moving quite close and regarding her severely.

Everyone waited to see what would happen. He could

have struck her with his stick, could have ordered the soldiers to take her away, but he just stood and looked at her instead – looked for so long that in the end she raised her eyes to his in a horrified stare. He shifted, glanced at her once more as though to say: "We'll be seeing each other yet" – and passed on to the boy's row.

Here his inspection went swift. He moved down the line with his hands on his back, swinging the stick; inspected the boys like a general reviewing his troops. Once or twice he saluted with a grin, but he stopped nowhere, said nothing. He seemed plainly satisfied.

Now he went to the children's hut. He gave an order for the door to be unlocked and went in – no doubt to inspect them as well, perhaps to put the Girl with the Cup on her feet, perhaps to comfort the crying ones. But no – he came out again right away, his handkerchief pressed to his face, coughing and gasping for air.

Two soldiers turned up carrying a huge bottle. Water! At last they would be given to drink. They were excited, impatient, but tried not to show it, not to annoy. They stood still, like the men in the row facing them, thirsty like them and, like them, waiting for water.

The soldiers with the big bottle went towards the hut. Well, naturally, the little ones came first – the Girl with the Cup and all the others inside that stifling hot place. They seemed to take an awfully long time over it, though. Just don't let the soldiers spend all the water on the little ones and leave nothing for them here.

When the soldiers came out at last, the bottle was half empty. There would be no more than a sip for each. They kept their eyes anxiously on the bottle, barely able to keep from rushing at it, forcing themselves to stay in place, to wait. They were all waiting: the children, and the soldiers in line, and the ones with the bottle – waiting for a word from the Soldier with the Golden Buttons. At last he gave a sign: the men with the bottle turned, and to everyone's amazement began pouring the liquid from the bottle all around the hut. It gave out a strong smell, tickling the nostrils and making their eyes water.

The children stirred uneasily. The Big Girl turned this way and that with a fearful, apprehensive look, as though seeking help, as though knowing something the others didn't, as though wanting to run, to fly, to act – but having to stay in line. She folded her arms, her eyes wandering, questioning...

The Soldier with the Golden Buttons walked to the hut.

Something flickered.

A match!

He dropped the burning match at the foot of the hut.

A small flame sprang up, grew, spread, began to snake round the bottom of the hut, circled it, and reappeared at the other side, enclosing the hut in a ring of fire. And suddenly it flared up, began to lick at the walls.

"No-o-o-o!" shrieked the Big Girl, and hurled herself at the hut.

"No, no, no!" she cried in despair, as though warding off blows, and with wildly swinging arms tried to fight her way through the wall of fire, which grew taller and fiercer by the moment. The flames twisted and hissed, swept and consumed. The Big Girl was rushing to and fro, vainly seeking a space, a gap in the blazing wall. A piece of burning timber fell at her feet and she jumped back instinctively.

A thin little voice came from the fire:

"Mama!"

"Esty!" cried the Big Girl and with a great sob threw herself at the blazing hut again.

A soldier came, pushed her away, and she fell, her dress caught fire. For a moment she did not notice, then seized a wooden board and began hitting at herself and her dress till she managed to beat out the flames. Her hands covering her face she staggered back to the row of children.

The children had not moved, stood wide-eyed and petrified at the horror of the burning hut. Only the sight of the Big Girl, the look in her eyes, her blackened hands, her singed dress, startled them out of their stupor. They tore in a body to the hut, snatched up planks, bits of tin and cardboard, removed a sweater, a hat, a shoe, and savagely beat at the flames, But the flames devoured everything and only shot up higher.

The door caved in with a tremendous crash, and they all ran over, hoping to see the children come rushing out, their arms ready to receive them.

But no one came out.

They strove to pierce the flames with their eyes, hushed one another to catch a sound, cried out the names of brothers, sisters, friends, scurried back and forth, horror turning to despair. And still, through the fire and smoke they cried out names:

"David! David!"

"Esty, Estika! Answer me! It's me, Hedy!"

"Sammy!"

"Nicole!"

And still they sought an opening, a way to break through the flames – running round the hut, tripping and stumbling.

All at once, the Big Girl stopped, raised both hands to silence the others. They listened: a weak voice sounded from the hut, barely audible over the crackle and roar of the flames, but for the children it was a summons – each deemed it the voice he was waiting to hear. Once more they attacked the fire, beat furiously at the flames, sobbed out the name of the little ones in there.

The Big Girl ran to the Soldier with the Golden Buttons.

"Make them put out the fire!" she pleaded.

"Put it out," she whispered in a choking voice.

"Put it out!" she screamed. "There are children in there, little children. My sister is in there. David is there. Sammy, Nicole... Put it out! Oh, put it out!"

But the Soldier with the Golden Buttons did not move did not look at her – as though he had not heard, as though she did not exist. He stood and watched the raging fire, swinging his stick, a gleam of satisfaction on his face.

The Big Girl grabbed his stick, pulled at it, repeated in one last, hoarse, hysterical wail!

"*Put it out*!!"

He pushed her away, brushed the sleeve with the gloved hand, threw her a look of distaste.

She stood before him, fastened her eyes upon his face, and her eyes seemed to discover something unspeakable there. Slowly she retreated, moved back as though this pleasant, handsome, clean face with its faintly curled lips contained all the horror of the carnage behind her.

Blindly she moved, stumbled against the children. They were standing in a close group, pressed against each other, speechless, their eyes fixed on the single spot – on the bars of the window, still stuck in their frame, and on the Girl with the Cup hanging there.

She was still alive. Her fingers opened and closed and she appeared to think she was climbing, through her body did not move. Her face was tense with the strain of trying to escape and not being able to. Everything on her was in flames. Her hair was like a torch growing from her head.

The star on her arm flared up, but its scorched shreds did not drop – they burnt into her arm and became a huge blister. Her dress was gone, and now the little lace combination was on fire, turning her whole body into one large wound. She seemed unaware of it, though, seemed to feel no pain at all, clung to the bars with the last of her strength, still holding the cup, and softly, endlessly repeating: "*Mutti... Mutti...*"

Suddenly she seemed electrified, as though her eye had caught a wondrous sight. Her strength seemed to return to her, and with her gaze on the distance she began to move, pull herself up on the white-hot bars. One elbow melted, fused into the bar as though part of it, but she felt nothing. With a smile on her face, her eyes fastened on some inexpressible glory, she looked radiant with happiness.

She stuck the hand with the cup through the bars and repeated in a whisper: "Mutti."

Then she fell silent, stopped moving. For a moment it seemed as if she had only paused to listen to some faraway voice, but little by little the children perceived she was dead. She looked like an old doll now, a torn, dirty, discarded doll that someone had flung against the bars. Her eyes remained open, and their glassy stare seemed to be fixed upon each of the children. It seemed to hold them, root them to the ground, till, almost as one, they grasped that what they had just seen was Death.

They turned, broke out running, not knowing where, only to get away from that window. They scattered in every direction and only Biba remained, unable to move, staring at the window as though mesmerized by the glassy eyes of the Girl with the Cup. She tried to tear herself away but couldn't, watched as the flames took over the whole window and devoured it along with the girl. And still Biba saw the glassy eyes – looking at her from the fire, behind the outstretched hand with the cup.

Then, as if stung, she, too, broke into a run – away, away from there. She ran as though possessed, as though running for her life, as though pursued by a pack of wolves.

Without warning she found the Soldier with the Golden Buttons standing before her. He was regarding her kindly, seemed about to speak to her, ask "What's wrong, little one?" – or perhaps adjust her star as before, caress her cheek. Biba glanced up at him questioningly, but then some obscure feeling made her move back. Suddenly she felt a loathing for him, and a great fear. She looked at him, at his handsome face, his elegant clothes, his golden buttons, and he seemed to grow before her eyes, to spread, tower, loom over her – bigger than the hut, bigger than the fire, his head already touching the sky, and his hands – his hands reaching for Biba. In a moment he would seize her by the throat!

She turned and ran. She wished to escape, hide, see no one any more, not the children, not the soldiers, not the sun, the day.

She found a large box full of old dirty papers, got in, burrowed under, pulled the papers over her head. She must get away from them, let no one see her, no one ever find her. She closed her eyes, and at once they were all back – here, with her, in this box, under the papers. One by one they came: the Soldier with the Golden Buttons, the Girl with the Cup, the children, the men, the burning hut, the heat and the thirst.

Suddenly there was no room in the box, she felt cramped, hemmed in. She knocked the paper away – and they were all gone. Perhaps they were only hiding, though. Perhaps they were behind her, waiting to pounce. She peered over her shoulder. No. She crouched down in the box again, shut her eyes, and promptly they were there again – pushing her back and forth between them, playing with her as with a ball.

She looked about her: there was the hut, no longer burning, but with a pall of evil-smelling smoke hanging over it. And there was the Soldier with the Golden Buttons, his big black boots seeming very near, seeming enormous, like the seven-league boots of the man-eating giant from the story. He had no club, was not covered in wolf's fur, his hair wasn't long and matted. He was tall and young and handsome – and more terrible than any giant.

She stepped out of the box, crawled round and hid behind it, sitting hunched, chin on knees. A thin pleading voice sounded in her ears:

"*Bitte – Wasser!*"

She opened her eyes to escape the voice but it would not go away, grew louder and louder, and it was a if a thousand Girls with a thousand Cups were dancing madly about her, screaming and screaming, "*Bitte – Wasser!*" – and thrusting their empty cups at her.

Five

The Big Girl was sitting alone on an upturned crate, staring blindly at the still warm ashes of the hut. It was quiet where she sat, almost peaceful, and gradually, one by one, the other children began to gather about her, popping up from under piles of paper, from behind boxes, cartons, garbage heaps. As though by prior agreement they all looked to the Big Girl, waiting for a word for her. She studied their faces as though searching for someone among them. At last, when they had all assembled, she rose, walked to the charred remains of the hut. The children followed, They started raking the ashes, digging, seeking – but all they could find was the girl's cup and a few blackened children's shoes, nothing more.

The Big Girl stood up and returned to her crate. Mutely the children followed, sat on the ground at her feet.

A trail of thin misty smoke rose from the embers, ascended in a delicate spiral to the sky, became a tiny cloud, a wisp in the wind, a whisper, a sigh. They followed it with their eyes till it dissolved.

Was it true, then? Had nothing remained? Nothing at all?

The heat grew worse. The sun above, the sand under their

feet – everything blazed. They were thirsty, so thirsty that now they could think of nothing else. They were faint with thirst, their body limp with it, their lips cleaving together till it needed an effort to open them. They sprawled on the sand, stupefied, dazed, the sun burning on their heads. Parched they were, thinking only of water, water.

A fair-haired boy pointed at something in the distance, his raised arm was the only moving thing in the inert mass of children. No one took notice of him. The boy, though, kept pointing insistently. He muttered something, his eyes searched dully for a child who would understand him. Two or three of those near him turned to look at him, mildly puzzled – but even so faint a sign of interest sufficed to encourage the blond boy. He rose to his knees, pointed again at the same distant spot. The children's eyes turned to look, but they saw nothing. The boy considered, then lifted his fist to his mouth in a drinking movement.

"Water," whispered the children.

Slowly, sluggishly, they stirred, moved their heavy limbs; and only when one of the children pronounced the word clearly again, "water," did excitement grip them.

One by one they stumbled to their feet, dragging themselves up with an effort, as though someone had told them not to leave this spot to which the sun had pinned them down. Then, as if at a sudden command, they broke into a run.

"Water!" each of them repeated to himself, "Water!"

There, somewhere in the distance, there was water. They must run, hurry to get there, get ahead of the others, get there first. Perhaps there wasn't much, perhaps not enough for all, perhaps even just a few drops, only enough for those who would get there first.

No, no, impossible, she, Biba, must drink too. She must hurry, hurry as fast as she can.

God, the Big Girl! If she gets there first she will drink it all up. She is big, she needs lot of water, and she can drink awfully fast. No, she is kind, she will leave some for the others. How about the rest of them; one of the bigger boys for instance who never talks but just sits? Look at them running! She must overtake them, trip them up, make them fall over a stone, a stick, just not let them get there before her. She must hold them back.

And as Biba ran she gave a push to someone who was trying to pass her. Never had she done such a thing before, but now she did not even look back to see if he had fallen. Who was that overtaking her now? Vlado. No doubt he would get there ahead of everyone. He could outrun them all. Look at him shoving everyone out of the way, hitting out with elbows and fists, knocking everyone down,. Oh, she must run, run, be in front, let no one catch up with her. She must reach the water as fast as she can and drink and drink. Only she. Only she must drink because she is thirstier than them all. She must drink all the water and not share it with anyone.

Very likely they were all thinking the same, for now they all seemed to gather strength, run even faster, run and shout: "Water! Wa-a-ter! Wa-a-ter!"

Their excitement mounted, ran as a wave through them all, and they raced, galloped, pushed, struck out savagely, their glazed eyes staring straight ahead of them. Each knew of nothing but himself, nothing but his own need.

Then they saw it: a large puddle. Briefly they paused, hesitated, but that movement was enough for the stragglers to catch up with them. That enraged the firstcomers, even alarmed them a little, and they flung themselves down, crawled to the puddle and began to drink.

Shortly there was no room left round the puddle and they started to fight, jostling for space, pinching, pulling hair, kicking, crying. Each wanted a place at the puddle, no one was ready to yield. Presently, even the slow ones managed to worm their way to the water somehow, and it grew quiet around the muddy, scum-covered pool. Nothing was heard but their sucking, gulping, coughing. They lapped up the water like puppies till they tasted mud in their mouths, till the puddle was drained to the bottom.

Biba got up. She wiped the mud from her lips, made to dry her hands on her dress but had mud all down the front. She looked about for a piece of paper, a rag, some grass, but her hands had already dried of their own.

She felt drained, felt a sort of numb unease, a mixture of shame and resentment. She was unwilling to raise her eyes, see the children, the puddle, anything. She wanted to be alone, turn her back on the others. She no longer cared for them, and knew they no longer cared for her.

They were all still there, sitting on the ground hugging their knees, or lying flat on their stomachs still, but they were no longer together – not like before, when they had gathered round the crate, not like on the train, listening to the Big Girl's stories. They would never again be as they were on the train – as they were that time when they had all joined to make the curtain round the bucket for the shy girl.

Now they sat each to himself, unable to look one another in the eye.

The Big Girl lay face down on the muddy ground. She was weeping softly, trying to stifle the convulsive sobs that shook her whole body.

In a moment they were all weeping, all of them, in great shuddering wails. Biba looked at them. She herself felt not the slightest desire to cry, nor any urge to comfort the others. It was as if they weren't there at all, as if she were seeing them through a glass wall. She wondered why they were crying.

Hadn't it happened once before that everyone had been crying except herself? Had it happened to her, though, or was it something she'd been told about? She made an effort to remember. Yes, it had been a long, long time ago: the images turned up before her eyes one by one, like pictures in an album she was idly leafing through:

Francka in the kitchen, burying her face in her apron, wandering about, stirring something in a saucepan, shaking her head and crying.

Aunt Lizinka putting on Biba's shoes for her, tears running down her white face.

Aunt Ksenija, also putting on her shoes, struggling with the laces on account of the tears in her eyes.

She looked up. There was Vlado, and the girl with the long braids, and the boy who had seen the water first – and they were all crying. All of them. Even the Big Girl. All except Biba.

Six

Soldiers arrived in a large truck, jumped down, unloaded a can of water and some loaves of bread. They shared it out, waited till all the children had eaten and drunk, then helped them up on the truck and drove off.

The children did not know where they were going, but for the time being it was enough to have soldiers with them again, to be led away from the site of the fire, away from the foul water, the sand, the heat, the thirst.

Silent with fatigue, they looked out through the open back of the truck. The place they had left was no longer in sight. They were driving past open country – grass, birds, sky. They didn't suppose the soldiers would mind if they went and stood by the open back, but they didn't feel like getting up. They were content to stay where they were, near the soldiers.

They were no longer thirsty, the heat had abated and a fresh breeze had sprung up, and that was all they cared for a moment.

Far away on the distant horizon the sun was setting.

The sun!

Once, in some infinitely remote past, the word "sun" had

meant something else entirely. It had meant a bright lovely day, chirping birds, gardens in bloom and wild flowers in the field, the ripple of golden corn, buds on the trees, windows flung wide, laughter, happiness...

Now they had come to know a different sun – a blazing sun, a fire-feeding sun helping flames to devour children, a sun that beat on one's head and blinded one's eyes and burnt one's lips and brought thirst – unbearable thirst.

They had come to know a sun that would hurt.

The sky blazed in a glory of crimson.

The truck stopped. They were neither surprised, nor alarmed, neither pleased or sorry. They knew that this trip would not last forever and that they were bound to arrive somewhere – and now they had. One by one they climbed down the iron rungs, reached the ground, found themselves beside two long lines of soldiers. The soldiers who had come with them went and formed a third line, at right angles to the other two. Without being told, as though out of long habit, the children, too, fell into line. They arranged themselves by size, starting with the Big Girl, and taking care to remain close to their own soldiers, to line up right in front of them. The truck drove off in a cloud of dust, churning the sand.

Now they had time to survey their new surroundings. They were standing at the edge of a vast square somewhat resembling an enormously large playground, the middle of which stood a tall hand-operated water pump, rather like pumps in railway stations. Their glances traveled beyond the square, and what they saw there made their blood run cold: it was a hut!

They did not notice the arrival of more soldiers, the braking of a small motorcar. They saw nothing but the hut – a large wooden hut with barred windows, just like...

Or perhaps it was that hut. Perhaps they were still there, waiting for water, and the hut was full of little children. Perhaps nothing had happened yet...

No, no. This hut was different. There was a pump here, and a square, and round the square more huts, and they were whole and looked almost new...

Besides, those huts were obviously inhabited. The whole place appeared inhabited, not like that other one. People live here...

Yes, but what of it? What if this hut was different? They would be driven inside anyhow, locked inside just like the little children before. And then the Soldier with the Golden Buttons would come, would give the order to pour liquid round the hut, would strike a match, and a little flame would spring up, grow, start its journey round the hut, rise and spread and become a blaze, a fire, from which there would be only one escape – the window with the white-hot bars.

"Oh, no!" whispered one of the children. They all turned to look at him: he stood frozen with terror, pointing at the corner of the square. The children followed the direction of his pointing finger with their eyes, and stiffened.

It was him – the Soldier with the Golden Buttons.

The girl standing next to Biba screamed and fled from the line. She was brought back, but her legs would not carry her. She slumped to the ground and crouched there, whimpering.

They looked at the tall approaching figure in its carefully

pressed uniform with its gold braid and its buttons, at the shiny boots, at the stick swinging behind its back. He threw them a glace, then turned on his heel and walked to the hut, followed by all their eyes.

A hush fell, broken only by the sand gritting under the soles of his boots as he strode calmly across the wide square. Tensely they watched every step, every move.

Oh, they knew what was going to happen. The door was going to open, and the soldiers behind them were going to push them towards it. Then they would close the door and set them on fire. Their hair would burn like a torch on their heads, their arms would become huge blisters, their clothes would blaze on their bodies – and by the window *he* would stand, the Soldier with the Golden Buttons. And he would be tall and fair and his lips would curl faintly in a smile.

Only a few steps remained between him and the hut.

Only a few steps, and then, and then...

But perhaps there already were children in the hut. Other children, like ones like the Girl with the Cup and Esty and David – like all the children the Big Girl had told her stories to... Perhaps they were there in that hut, crying – or laughing and playing, unaware of the evil approaching them, of the Soldier with the Golden Buttons, of the match in his hand, the little flame...

Now he had reached the hut. He raised his head, slid the bolt, opened the door, and then –

A huge dark lump burst from the hut, a screaming and wailing mass of monstrous creatures. Screaming, they swept past the Soldier with the Golden Buttons – pushing and shoving, trampling down the fence, raising a cloud of dust, looking right nor left as they raced for the square.

Stunned, the children watched the wild swarm advance upon them. It was coming fast – a mass of flailing arms, kicking legs; jostling, tripping over each other, trampling fallen bodies, open mouths shrieking – a raging menace converging on them.

The children grasped each other by the hand and drew back against the line of the soldiers behind them.

The mob was nearly upon them. With a shock the children saw that it was made of women without hair or teeth, dressed in rags, eyes gaping out of bruised and swollen faces. Like a nightmare they came, hands outstretched, reaching for the children, about to seize them in their clutches.

The children ducked, clung to the soldiers' boots, sought refuge between them, crouching low, hiding their faces.

The women in front stopped, holding back the others, and as they tried to break through, women in front linked arms and formed a barrier to keep them from advancing. They stood, and slowly the huge cloud of dust they had made began to settle.

The first women moved slowly forward again. They were calmer now, more in control of themselves, restraining tears and groans.

And then, in a low stunned voice, one boy whispered: "Mama?"

The other children looked at him, at the women, and back at him again, as though he must be a criminal or a beggar to have a mother like that. How could he, how could *any* child, have a woman like that for a mother?

Biba was looking down, away from the boy, away from the women. It was such a long time since she had heard anyone say "Mama". She closed her eyes, tried silently to repeat the magic word that was bringing tears to her eyes. She felt happy just to think the word. She would have like to be somewhere else now, to be alone so that she could say it aloud without anyone hearing her: "Mama".

She looked up, and the mob was still there. She felt threatened, as if expecting a blow, wanted to run away, but stayed where she was.

A pair of arms reached out for her, and a cracked woman's voice, trembling with emotion, whispered:

"Biba..."

She started.

No one had called her that for so long that she had almost forgotten it applied to her. She tried to remember the last time that anyone had called her by that name. It was a long time ago, so long that she had to think very hard to recall it. At some railway station it had been, on a platform with many soldiers. There had been a crowd of people making their way through trunks, parcels, boxes; a crowd of shouting and weeping people. She herself had been standing by the open door of a big railway car and had seen her mother in the grip of two soldiers – struggling with them, trying to free herself. They had pushed her on roughly, though, pulled her by the hair, struck her; but before she had vanished beyond the door with the star, she had cried one last time, at the top of her voice: "Bi-ba!"

It was the same voice that was calling her name now.

Biba kept her hands in front of her face and tried to

burrow even deeper in among the soldier's boots. Through her fingers she peered at the woman. Now the woman dropped to her knees, held out two dirty, shaking hands, inched a little closer – so close that Biba could almost feel her breath on her face.

Cautiously she spread her fingers a little, studied the grimy, tear-streaked face, the hairless skull, the bruises, the black-and-blue marks. She tried to compare this fact to some other, familiar one, but try as she would found no trace of resemblance. The woman was watching her expectantly, made to say something with the puffed lips, but gave up – humbled, weeping.

Presently the woman recovered, raised her eyes, moved till her knees met Biba's feet, lifted a hand to touch her, but Biba flinched, shrank back to avoid her. The woman withdrew her hand at once, clapped it to her mouth to stifle a low moan, and said in a barely audible voice:

"Biba, my little Biba, don't you know me?"

Biba saw the tears running down the woman's cheeks, trickling to her chin, her throat, leaving trails on the dusty skin – and suddenly she felt a sort of closeness, an affection, a sense of affinity. Somehow she felt that she belonged to this woman here and to no other woman whatever. Her mind formed a picture of Francka and of Aunt Ksenija and Aunt Lizinka, and there seemed to be a connection between all those faces and this one here before her.

The woman made an effort to smile at her, then heaved a sigh. "So long as you're alive," she whispered. "Alive... here... Oh, Biba, by darling..." She seemed to want to take Biba in her arms, but as Biba was still avoiding her she dropped her hands, mumbled: "It's all right... it's all right..."

The soldier stirred. Slowly, carefully, he pulled his boots from under Biba's body. She was forced to get up. Deprived of her shelter, she stood, lost and lone and defenseless, before the woman who must, presumably, be her mother. She no longer tried to hide or escape. Passively she allowed the woman to carry her away.

Seven

Three days had passed, and still Biba slept. Once in a while she would wake up, blink sleepily, but before she could come properly awake her eyelids would droop again and she slept on, with the gaze of the hairless woman upon her. Each time she caught sight of the woman, of her face and large eyes, she seemed more familiar, rousing distant memories of something that could only be recaptured if she closed her eyes, hovered between sleep and wakefulness.

The woman was there now, rising from the great whirling cloud of dust. No, not dust – smoke. Black smoke carrying the stench of burning flesh and paper and garbage. There is a watchful raven there, and a scavenger dog sniffing at the garbage, but except for them the hairless woman is alone. Everyone had gone away and left her, and she is raking the ashes and wandering about as though searching for the others, trying to understand why they have all gone, where they all are. They were here, just a moment ago, right here, all of them, all the little children from the train – the Girl with the Cup and the golden-haired girl crying for her mummy and Esty and David and Nicole... They were here just a moment ago, so how are they suddenly gone? Gone where?

They had nowhere to go. The woman turns over boxes, sifts through the ash, looks for traces, relics, anything.

She has found something. She picks it up, turns to Biba and holds it out to her as though it were an immensely precious object, but before Biba can take it a mob of wailing shrieking figures appears out or nowhere. They converge on the hairless woman like a surging wave and she vanishes under their feet. They trample her savagely with their bare feet and she turns all flat, turns into a dirty scrap of cardboard lying in the mud...

Biba gave a start. Her eyes opened, wandered unseeing about the room. She seemed to waver – as though wishing to flee some great danger, but wondering whether she wasn't about to land herself into an even greater one. She moistened her lips with the water someone was holding for her, felt the touch of a hand and knew there was someone beside her but refused to look, not wanting to see, afraid of what her eyes might find. She was tired, heavy, wanted to sleep. She heard a child's whimper, sounding near and at the same time vary far away, a child moaning "Mama!"

"Mama," Biba repeated to herself. "Mama, mama," she whispered soundlessly, like a lullaby rocking her to sleep.

She strained to open her eyes, but her eyelids closed and she dropped into sleep again, into silence and darkness and fog. Then the fog lifted and revealed a large barren waste – miles and miles of arid land where grass had grown once but had been burnt to death by the sun. There was a swamp in the middle of it – a festering wound on a pale body. Smoke rose from the swamp as from a volcano, and the children were lying around it. No, not actually lying, but sort of floating round it, turning like some huge chandelier ornamented with bronze angels. They were trying to reach their mouths to the swamp, but whenever they were on the point of succeeding, someone came and pulled them back. Biba knew she was dreaming. She tried to turn over, to banish the nightmare. She came half awake, heard a whispered conversation by her bed –

"Still asleep?"

"Yes. And her pulse is so faint. I can't feel it at all sometimes, and then I think she is dying here before my eyes and there is nothing I can do. So terribly weak as she is. She has eaten nothing for three days, just slept and slept."

"Don't worry, she'll be all right. Let her sleep all she needs."

"If only I knew what she's been though all this time! Have any of the other children said a word?"

"No. Some are sleeping, too, and the rest say nothing..."

Biba is falling, falling. She is falling into an abyss, and in the next moment she is floating high up in the air. Then she is back on the railway platform. People are pushing and shoving. A great crowd, all in a hurry to get somewhere. Some are proper travelers, some belong to the train, and all the rest are soldiers. Biba runs, wants to hide, because now they are chasing her, but they mustn't catch her, they mustn't, because she has to find the door with the star where Mama is. She can hear her shouting, louder than the engine, louder than the crowd, the loudspeaker – louder than anything, her mother's voice shouting:

"Give me my child! My child! Bi-ba!"

And Biba runs, past people, trunks, soldiers – runs and

cries: "Mama! Ma-ma-a!..." She arrives just as the soldiers are pushing Mama inside, just as Mama holds out a hand to her and shouts "Biba!" – and is gone.

Now the soldiers are coming for Biba. She tries to avoid them, and gradually consciousness returns and she knows it's a dream and forces herself to wake up.

She opened her eyes wide, stared at the ceiling, tried to make herself see nothing, tear herself out of the grip of those terrifying images. She made an effort to think of something else, something beautiful, something far away and long ago. She tried to form a picture of mountains, sunlight, flowers in green meadows, blue skies with birds flying in them, and butterflies... Butterflies flitting over the meadow, settling on flowers. She is chasing them with a net, wants to catch one, but they always fly off just when she thinks she has caught them. Flushed, panting, she perseveres. In her starched white dress, lace-edged petticoat, silk ribbons in her hair, she looks like a big butterfly herself. Everyone is out to help her in her chase, just as in a fairytale: the tall grass bends to show her which way to go, the trees dip their branches at her, offering the slender twigs whereon the butterflies have landed, lovely like a mass of brilliant flowers. Holding her breath, she tiptoes nearer, lifts the net high and – whoops! – two large and splendid butterflies are caught in her net.

Elated, she sets off at a run to the mansion, calling from afar:

"Mama, Mama! I caught two! I caught two!"

Mama appears on the balcony, laughing, her long fair

hair blowing in the wind. She waves both hands to Biba, signals that she is coming to meet her. And when Biba climbs the hill, out of breath, she comes running towards her, silk dress frou-frouing, hair flying, arms out to Biba – Mama, lovely as a picture.

Together they look at the butterflies, and the butterflies look at them. And Mama tells her a butterfly is transformed out of a plain caterpillar; how many legs a butterfly has; how come its wings are so fragile and colourful; what this thin dusty stuff on it is for; why some butterflies are dotted and some striped; how long a butterfly lives, and where its eyes are. Then, when she knows all there is to know about butterflies, they open the net and set them free, gaze after them till they have quite disappeared, blended with the grass and the flowers and the sky, become one with the fields and clouds.

Her eyes opened and met the glance of the hairless woman. She did not turn away but kept her eyes fixed on the woman's face, and the longer she looked the more it seemed to remind her of something. She felt oddly moved, yet ashamed of her feeling and unwilling to show it. The woman was looking at her expectantly, seemed about to speak, to ask her something, and Biba decided she had better close her eyes again to avoid whatever it might be. But as soon as her eyes closed, sleep came and with it the harrowing scenes...

The hairless woman is on her knees before Biba. With both hands she tries to shield a chunk of bread, to save it for Biba. Her bruised face is wet with tears, and her tired cracked voice repeats monotonously:

"Biba, Biba, my little Biba, don't you know me? It's me, Mama!"

Biba draws back, hugs the soldier's boots, peers out from behind them. And when everyone has gone away, soldiers and children, and only she and the woman are left face to face, the woman whispers once more, very gently, lovingly:

"It's me, my darling, it's Mama!"

She woke up. This time she felt that it was for good, that she wouldn't fall asleep any more, but she kept her eyes shut, wishing to be ready for the moment when, wide awake, she would meet the questioning glance of the woman sitting by her bed. She made an effort to remember where she was, what the room she was in looked like, who the woman was; tried to accustom herself to the idea that there were other women and children in the room, and that *this* woman was her mother. It was quite pleasant to lie like that with closed eyes, but she knew she couldn't keep it up forever. She opened her eyes.

Her glance fell on the ceiling, traveled over the wooden walls, examined the room at her leisure, as though she had all the time in the world. At last her eyes came to rest on her mother, and she sat up politely and forced a smile. Her mother settled her back, smoothed the sackcloth blanket and offered her a cup of water. Biba drank, avoiding her mother's eyes, returned the cup and said hoarsely:

"Thank you!"

"Praise God!" sighed her mother, sinking onto the edge of her bed. "She speaks!"

Biba looked at her curiously. She felt sorry for her, felt she ought to stroke the shaven head, touch the poor bruised face, say something. She might ask *why* they had shaved her head, who had bruised her face, but she'd only tell her what Biba could guess for herself. The soldier had done it – shaved them, beaten them, left them without water. Maybe they, the women, had also drunk at the puddle like the children, had also tried to save others from the flames. That's the way things were here.

Her mother must be waiting for her to do or say something. What, though? What could she say to her?

Her mother swallowed, smiled at her:

> "You slept and slept. I was beginning to think you were ill. How do you feel now?"

Biba went on looking at her as though she had not heard the question, slowly running eyes over her mother's face, studying it intently. Her mother, embarrassed, put out a hand, touched Biba's hair, shyly caressed her cheek, asked anxiously:

> "Have I changed that much? Yes, I'm not surprised you didn't recognize me at first. I must look like a monster... But you know, so many things..."

Her voice trailed off and she bowed her head. She had been on the point of telling Biba about the many things that had happened to her, then thought better of it – for who knew what had happened to Biba? What infinitely worse things than to her? Perhaps she *would* never know. She looked up, saw the quiet compassion in Biba's eyes, and realized that indeed, she *would* never know. Whatever it was that had happened to Biba had put up a barrier between them, and she would never be able to breach it. For a long time she said nothing, and it was Biba who broke the silence at last.

"And Papa?" she asked softly.

"They sent him away, I don't know where. I haven't seen or heard from him since that night they came for us. They separated us that night, and took each to a different place... I never thought I'd see either of you again – you, or Papa... But now at least we two are together. Now at least I have you back... alive... here... I never thought... Oh, but you'll see, everything will be all right. My face will heal, and my hair will grow, and then everything will be as it was before, won't it?"

Biba said nothing. What was there to say? She wished her mother would keep silent too, but her mother talked on and on. Biba gave an impatient little toss of her head, but as that didn't stop her, Biba tried to get up.

"No, my darling, you mustn't," said her mother. "You're not strong enough yet, your legs won't carry you. You must stay in bed a little longer."

Biba smiled a little, as though in resignation, as though saying: "Ah, well, if you say I must..." Obediently she lay back, keeping the hand with the blisters away from her mother. She pulled the blanket up, asked for some water. Obviously pleased to do something for her, her mother lifted the cup and brought it to Biba's lips, but Biba took it firmly from her hands, refused to be babied.

Her mother apparently still needed to talk:

"Everything will be all right, you'll see. Everything will

be all right... But now you should eat something. You're weak, you must eat all you can. There, bread – that's all I have. Do you want it?"

"Yes, please."

Her mother was beginning to talk again, was going to tell her a story perhaps, but after a word or two she paused and stared openmouthed at Biba nibbling her bread, eating it crumb by careful crumb, one hand under the chin to catch falling crumbs. Where had she learnt to eat her bread that way? When? Who had taught her? Only camp inmates ate like that. Could she have acquired camp habits so fast? And did it mean that henceforth they would be like companions – two fellow prisoners with the same prison habits and the same duties?

Once more it was Biba who broke the silence.

"Shall we be living here now?" she asked, not because she did not know the answer, but to offer her mother an opening.

"Yes, in this hut, with some of the other mothers and children. You already know a few of the children, don't you? You'll soon meet the rest as well, and then you can play with them when I'm away at work. And listen, Biba – you have to be very good when I'm away. There are soldiers everywhere, and you must do exactly as they tell you."

Biba lay and listened to her mother, but her eyes seemed to say: "I know. Please, I know all that, and so much more besides."

The women in the hut were preparing to leave. Her mother rose:

"I must go to work now. I'll be back late in the

afternoon. Will you wait for me here, or go out to play with the other children?"

"I'll wait here."

"All right."

Her mother was watching her, searching her face. Had there been a flicker in Biba's eyes? A hint of something? Had she been going to speak? Didn't her look say that she was happy they were together again? Could she take Biba in her arms now? No, no, she must be patient.

"I'm going now. Bye-bye!"

"Bye-bye!" said Biba nicely.

At the door her mother glanced back one more time – waiting, hoping. Was there nothing in Biba's face? Hadn't she caught a tiny glint there? A sign she was going to speak? To say, for instance:

"Come back soon, Mama!" – or

"I'll be waiting for you, Mama, don't be late!" – or:

"Don't go, Mama, stay just a bit longer" – or...

As soon as the door closed behind her mother, Biba slipped out of bed and tiptoed to the window to see her pass. She caught sight of her just as she turned the corner round the hut to avoid a soldier, and again when she emerged on the other side. And only when she felt sure no one could see her, only then did Biba quickly press her face against the screen, lift a hand and send her mother a greeting.

Eight

A new life began.

They would rise at dawn to queue up for their water ration: each person was allowed one cup, which had to last him the day. The women had learnt to thrust their tin cups quickly, one after the other, under the flowing spout without wasting a drop. Even so it would happen that the pump ran dry before the last in line had reached it, and then the other women would each contribute a spoonful of their own ration, since no one could survive without water in that heat.

Returning to the hut, they would make their beds, sweep the floor, and wash their faces – all in the same tub that was meant to serve three huts. Next they would carry out the bodies of those who had died in the night, and a few women would gather round to say the Kaddish prayer for the dead in a low, hurried mumble, before the bodies would be carted away. They would go about this whole routine quietly, efficiently, as a matter of course.

A blast of the siren announced the morning roll-call. They lined up outside in front of their huts, mothers and children, and the soldiers came and counted them, removed the weak, the sick and the dead and piled them all upon the same cart, seeing that the same fate awaited them anyhow.

Sometimes the soldiers would read out some proclamation or other, mete out some punishment, and leave.

The *Kapo* determined which women would join which working party. Occasionally they sent the children to work as well, but as a rule they remained in the huts.

The camp was situated in a hot, airless valley hemmed in by low hills and forests. The country round it, beyond the high barbed-wire fence, grew lush with green and flowers, making the camp grounds itself look like a clearing from which all grass and trees had deliberately been pulled up to turn it into a patch of desert.

The huts were built in a close ring round the large sandy, shadeless square. A few tall trees had been left to stand in the space near the camp entrance, which, with its little white houses and low wooden fence, was strictly out of bounds to the camp inmates. One boy had strayed past the sign warning off trespassers one day, and his body had been exhibited during roll-call as a lesson to them all.

Once in a while some officers would show up, and you could always foretell their coming well in advance. The soldiers were tenser than usual, the guards were stricter, and the *Kapo* would inspect every bed in case it concealed a sick woman who had escaped detection, would peer into the women's faces for signs of failing strength, would search every corner. No officers' visit ever passed without the removal of some body from the hut. The slightest sign of resistance, real or imagined, would entail severe punishment.

Once an officer happened to catch a sight of a girl who was refusing to give her mother a hand. He went over and fixed his eyes on the child, and she stared back at him rigid with fear, unable to look away, lower her eyes.

"So?" he screamed. "You don't want to give her a hand? If you don't want to give her hand – it means you don't love her. If you don't love her – maybe you'd like to beat her, what? Here, take this stick and beat her, then. Beat her! Beat her, I tell you!"

The girl clasped her hands tightly behind her back and recoiled in horror. But the officer forced the stick into her hand, shook her roughly by the shoulder, and kept demanding that she beat her mother. The mother herself bent and offered her back to the child, urging her gently to comply:

"Beat me, beat me, my darling, my sweet love. Don't be afraid. I know you don't mean it. Beat me, please, beat me. He'll kill you if you don't. Quick, before he gets angry!"

The girl grasped the stick, hit her mother once and pulled back her hand as if stung. But the officer did not let go – he pushed and kicked her till, in a sudden panic, she seized the stick and began raining blows on the mother's back. The officer stood over her, shouting:

"More, more, harder! That's it! More!"

Whenever she paused even briefly the officer would at once lash out at her, slapping the girl's face, kicking her. Then, as suddenly as she had begun, she stopped. She flung her stick to the ground and gently helped her mother up. They took her away.

Sometimes the Soldier with the Golden Buttons paid

them a visit as well. On those occasions he would nearly always pause by the door of Biba's hut and glance in at her and the other children who had come in her group. He always looked his own elegant self – unfailingly cheerful, handsome in his pressed uniform, his gold braid. At roll-call he like to linger before their row, review each child's face as though to check if they were all still there.

One day he appeared in the company of a fat old roundcheeked officer. They made straight for the Big Girl who was standing there all by herself. She had no one left in the camp: her little sister Esty had been burnt with the others in the hut, and her mother had been taken away one morning during roll-call. They eyed her, told her to turn round and raise her skirt. They consulted each other, and at last the fat officer nodded and the soldiers came and took her. She went quickly, unresisting, as though prepared – not glancing back once.

Mutely they watched the proceedings, only asking themselves as they fell into line: "Who will be next? Me, perhaps?"

Mornings the mothers would leave for work, and all day the children would wait for their return. They could have played, told each other stories, got up a bit of mischief – but they seemed to have forgotten how. Mostly they hung about the huts waiting for their mothers.

Their numbers kept steadily dwindling, reducing those who shared a common language even further. Not that it bothered them much: they spoke so little that it scarcely seemed to matter. Chattering, playing – it seemed silly and childish.

117

Biba could have sought Vlado's company, but as time passed Vlado grew more and more sullen. He generally preferred to sit somewhere by himself, looking moody and somber. On the rare occasions when they did talk, they avoided the subject of mothers. Vlado's mother was alive, actually, but she lived in a house instead of a hut and her hair had not been shorn. She would come to see him sometimes, but he was never glad with her visits. He had told Biba once that he did not love his mother because she wouldn't live with him like the other children's mothers.

Weeks passed and became months, and the months followed each other and it was summer again. A full year had gone by since their arrival – and Biba's mother was growing thinner and weaker by the day. She hardly ever talked now. She would return from work completely exhausted – always bringing half a slice of bread for Biba, explaining it was a prize for having done her job particularly well. Biba would receive this gift gladly – both because she was hungry and because she knew it pleased her mother to be doing something for her.

The fact was that Biba had grown to love her mother – and that she could not bring herself to show it. In the morning she would follow her stealthily to work, always afraid something might happen to her on the way. Often she would squat somewhere out of sight, stay there for hours in the sun, secretly watching her mother, ready to rush to her aid if anything should happen.

It was on one such occasion she discovered that the bread her mother brought her was part of her daily ration, and not a prize for good work. Reluctant to reveal she had found her out, Biba said nothing, but henceforth she pretended to be less hungry and shared the bread with her mother. With a heart full of love and anxiety she would watch her mother raise a tired, trembling hand to her mouth to eat it.

They shared the same bed, or rather – wooden board resting on two crates, with some coarse sacks doing duty for mattress and blanket. The board was so narrow and the sacks so few that it forced them to lie huddled close together. Every night at bedtime Biba would be filled with apprehension, afraid her mother might embrace, kiss or caress her; or worse – want to talk to her, ask her about things she didn't wish to speak of. Every night, therefore, she would quickly lie down, close her eyes at once and pretend to be asleep. Her mother never did embrace her, though, and Biba was well aware of the effort it must cost her and was deeply grateful. And when her mother fell asleep, Biba would open her eyes again and lie looking at the harrowed face beside her.

Never since the day they had met had Biba called her "Mama", though every night before going to sleep she would promise herself that tomorrow morning she would get up, smile cheerfully and say in a perfectly natural voice: "Good morning, Mama!" But a full year had passed and Biba had not managed to keep her promise.

A morning came when her mother barely passed the roll-call. The Kapo eyed her suspiciously, and somehow she managed to pull herself together and stay on her feet, with Biba's surreptitious support. Biba could feel her mother shaking, could sense the effort it demanded of her to keep standing, or even just to take air into her lungs. If only she

119

could have led her back to the hut, put her to bed and looked after her.

The soldiers were gone, the women were leaving for work, and Biba's mother still stood there as though she could not make up her mind to move. She said nothing, but her face was wet with perspiration and Biba knew she was in pain.

She walked her to the laundry, sat on a rock outside, waiting. Whenever she heard the swish of the birch she would leap up and peer through the keyhole. No, it wasn't her mother. The thin back in its faded gray dress was still bent over the sink, and that was all that mattered to Biba. She returned to her rock, waited.

Once in a while the door would open, making Biba jump aside to avoid detection. A soldier emerged, threw an inert body on the sand, rang a bell and returned to the laundry-hut, without waiting for the soldier with the cart to collect the body. Biba waited till the door had closed behind him, then made a dash for the body before the other soldier should come. She heaved a sigh of relief, but watched the frail back with increased vigilance.

Towards nightfall the door opened wide and the women came out.

Biba ran to meet her mother. She wanted to hug her, lay her cheek against her mother's and whisper in her ear, "Mama, Mami..." – but was ashamed to. Her mother leaned against the doorpost, looked at Biba's face, and her eyes filled with gratitude for what she saw there. Supporting herself on Biba's shoulder, she let her lead her to the hut the way once, a long time ago, Biba had allowed her mother to take her there.

Nine

All night Biba watched by her mother's bedside. Whenever she nodded off for a moment she would come to with a start, terrified of what might have happened in the meantime, and looked at her mother's restlessly tossing figure. Now her mother would shiver with cold, now burn with fever and search blindly about her for the water cup, but her head would fall back heavily before she could moisten her lips, and she would doze off again.

"Let her sleep," thought Biba. "But when she wakes up in the morning she'll be thirsty. I've got to get to the pump ahead of everybody, make sure of a full cup." Softly she rose, moved on tiptoe past the row of beds, slipped out and closed the door behind her.

It was still dark outside, and for a while she stood there uncertainly, a little flustered by the utter silence, the darkness, the empty square, looking so much vaster than by day. She saw the silhouette of the guard, waited for him to move away, then sprinted across the square to the water-pump in the middle and sat with her ear against it, listening for the gurgle that would announce the first flow.

She thought of her mother. What was she doing now?

Perhaps she had woken up and was looking for Biba, worried by her absence? Or maybe she was all hot again and would feel better if Biba were there to wipe the sweat off her forehead? Maybe she felt sick, wanted to get up and there was no one to help her? Or wanted to drink and the cup was gone? She must be thirsty, terribly thirsty. And what if she wouldn't be able to get up in the morning, and the Kapo took her number? Maybe she had already been cast on the pile before the hut... No, no, impossible, she had been sleeping when Biba had left just a few minutes ago. But what if she should faint during roll-call, collapse in a heap at the soldier's feet? Or pass it all safely – hut inspection and the Kapo and roll-call – and then not come out of the laundry tonight?

What was happening there in the hut? Was she asleep? Were the other women asleep? Was she awake? And what if she were neither asleep nor awake but... No! she jumped up, ran a few steps and then checked herself, her eyes on the iron pump – cold and dead as if no water would ever flow through it.

Dawn broke. From the huts – black squares standing out sharply against the morning mist – the first shadowy figures of women and children emerged. From all sides they converged upon the pump as by an age-old routine, fell mutely into line behind Biba, and waited.

More and more people arrived and the line grew and twisted all across the square to the huts.

The pump was coming to life, coughing and spluttering in the morning stillness. A first dribble came out.

Biba held her cup under the spout, filled it to the brim

and moved carefully past the queue, back to the hut.

A woman from the another hut stopped her.

"How is Mother?" she asked.

"She's asleep."

"Will she be able to get up for roll-call?"

"I don't know," whispered Biba, a sudden tremor in her voice.

The woman sent her a probing look, then with a swift, resolute gesture thrust something into the pocket of Biba's dress.

"There!" she said. "My little Rivkah has no use for it any longer. Hide it, though."

Biba lowered her eyes. She knew that what the woman had given her was a medicine that had been intended for Rivkah, and that last night the women had gathered round Rivkah's bed and pulled the sacking over her face.

They had been friends, she and Rivkah. Some days they had waited together in front of the laundry for their mothers to finish work. She had not seen her all morning yesterday, and had gone to look for her in the hut. Rivkah had lain there with her eyes on the ceiling, not speaking, just smiling sweetly at anyone who came to see her, as though in apology, as though to say she was sorry but she didn't quite feel like talking just now. When her mother came with the pills at night – God only knew where she'd got hold of them, maybe stolen them from the pocket of the Soldier with the Golden Buttons – all that was left for her to do was to cover her daughter's face.

Biba would have liked to say something to her, but didn't know what. Their eyes met in a glance of understanding, and the woman whispered through her tears: "Hurry, before it's too late."

"Before it's too late, too late, too late" – the words rang through her head as she strode swiftly to the hut, carefully balancing the cup. Rivkah's mother had come too late. And she? Would she be in time? If only she could run, fly, if a miracle would happen – she'd be touched by a magic wand and find herself by her mother's bedside. If only she didn't have to walk, cross half the square, wondering, asking herself what she would find in the hut. But what could have happened? It was just a fever, and she'd just drink some water and feel better right away. Only hurry and get to her fast and spill nothing.

She arrived. Everyone was already up. The room monitor was checking the beds, pencil and paper in hand. Here and there she would cover up a face, write down the numbers of the sick and the spent – of anyone who wouldn't make it to the roll-call, who would be picked up by the soldier with cart.

The monitor had just reached her mother's bed. She was about to add her to the list when Biba rushed up to her.

"No!" she shouted. "She's only asleep!" She didn't dare look at the bed for fear of being disproved, but stared boldly into the monitor's eyes.

The monitor felt her mother's pulse, cast a dubious look at her ashen face, and warned Biba:

"Just so long as she turns up for roll-call! I shall get it if she doesn't."

"She will, she will, you'll see," Biba declared confidently. The monitor left. Biba felt her knees go weak and slumped against the bed, shutting her eyes for a moment, still afraid to look. How could she have promised that her mother would show up for roll-call without even knowing how she was? The first women were starting to leave, and she realized she hadn't much time left. She put the cup down, turned to the bed: her mother was lying quite still, her pale features showing no sign of life. She tried her pulse, thought she could detect a faint flutter, but wasn't sure – perhaps it was only that she so much wanted to feel it. No, no, it was there. In that case, she was asleep. Yes, asleep.

How to wake her? Call her. Yes, but how? Call her how? She couldn't just say "Mama" like that. She had never called her "Mama". But then how to wake her? She'd have to hurry, it was late, more and more women were leaving.

The monitor appeared in the doorway, threw her a suspicious glance, raised her pencil. Alarmed, Biba seized her mother by the shoulders, shook her. Her mother woke up with a start, a dazed look in her eyes, only half conscious yet, not clear about her surroundings. She saw Biba, tried to raise her head, say something, then dropped back in exhaustion, closed her eyes. Terrified she would fall asleep again, Biba jumped up, shouted:

"Mama!"

She had said it without thinking, startled by her own voice.

But her mother's eye opened, went to the ceiling as though she were listening intently to something, not sure whether she had heard it or not. Slowly her face turned to Biba, and her large eyes were radiant with happiness. She made to say something, but burst into tears instead.

She cried softy, without a sound, her hands over her face

– cried and cried as if to cleanse herself of all the pain, all the unspoken words.

Biba knelt beside her. There was nothing she wanted so much now as to throw her arms around Mama, bury her face against her shoulder and tell her how much she loved her. Instead of which she said, irrelevantly:

"Maybe today we'll have a letter from Papa."

Mama took her hands away from her face and looked lovingly at her little Biba. Gently she touched her flushed cheek and whispered:

"Maybe."

Now Biba knew that Mama would get up, and she became all practical.

"I've brought you water and some pills," she announced, as though it were the simplest thing – one just opened the medicine cupboard, took out some pills, turned on a tap and filled a cup.

Mama regarded the pills in astonishment but asked nothing. She put them on her tongue, drank some water, but after a few sips returned the cup to Biba, though clearly still thirsty.

"Have some more," Biba urged, "there's plenty."

Mama lay back, looked at Biba. It was the first time she had looked at her so openly, so frankly. Biba withstood the look and kept her own eyes on Mama's face, waiting, aware that there was something Mama wished to say – something she could say only now.

"You've grown so much."

At that instant the siren went off. The last women were hurrying out.

"Can you get up?" Biba asked anxiously.

"Yes."

Slowly, supporting herself against walls and beds, helped by Biba, she moved to the door. The sight of the Kapo and soldiers outside seemed to give her strength. She was still looking terribly pale, and Biba pinched her cheeks as she had often seen other women do. They had to wait a long time that day, longer than ever, but when the soldiers came Mama stood there upright and smiling before them, her cheeks fresh and rosy as though she had just returned from a holiday in the mountains. Biba pressed her hand triumphantly, and when the soldiers left they grinned happily together at the success of their deception.

Relieved though she was, Biba still wondered whether her mother would be able to stand a full day's work at the laundry. Her heart missed a beat whenever the laundry door opened, and as soon as it closed she would run and peer through the keyhole, watch the soldier in there, sure that if he were to strike Mama with the birch or kick her, Mama would collapse and her body would be flung on the sand. She winced at the mere thought of her mother, so fearfully weak still, receiving a stroke of the birch.

She heard a dull sound within – a blow? a falling body? – pressed her eye against the keyhole. At that instant Mama turned, looked at the door as though sensing Biba's presence beyond it, and laughed a little to herself. Biba's heart swelled with happiness: Mama was laughing! Good! She was laughing. She had recovered her strength and her spirits. The pills must have worked then. Everything was all right: Mama was laughing.

It was hot, the kind of day when the sun seems to press down on you, to drain you of all your energy. Biba left her rock and began to walk up and down along the tall barbed-wire fence behind the laundry hut, looking across at the green fields beyond. She decided to stay there for a bit, found her favorite spot where the large white daisies grew on the other side of the fence, and sat on the ground.

She would come here often to look at the daisies, to see if they had grown, if no one had picked them yet. They were particularly lovely today – large and shiny and in full bloom.

Her eyes went dreamily beyond them in the fields, to the wide valley rising slowly to meet the distant hills.

"Remember?" Mama had said to her one day when they passed this spot. "White daisies. You always used to pick me some for my birthday."

Biba had often thought of her mother's words since. She had tried to remember, but it was all so dim, that other world, so remote and beyond grasp. She sometimes thought it never had existed, that there had always been only the camp, that she had never known any other people except soldiers and camp inmates. And yet Mama had said it lightly, smilingly, as though it were quite as real as this camp before her eyes: "Don't you remember? White daisies? You always used to pick me some for my birthday."

But Biba did not remember. She stared out over the green fields, breathed the smells of earth and flowers coming from there – and they reminded her of nothing. All she could see was the reality before her: barbed-wire, and beyond it the fields and the daisies. It evoked nothing – least of all Mama's birthday.

Mama! She jumped up, rushed to look through the keyhole, but Mama wasn't there. The spot where she had been standing before was taken up by a large wooden tub. Biba was just about to panic, to think that the worst had happened, when she caught sight of Mama out of the corner of her eye. They had moved her to another job, and she was now standing by a table and folding linen. Biba drew a long breath. She supposed this work was easier – Mama didn't have to stoop so much, she could probably lean against the wall from time to time, and if she were lucky perhaps even sit down for a bit. She lingered on briefly, making sure Mama was all right, then returned to her post on the rock.

She was tired, felt like sleeping, but dared not leave the laundry and go to the hut. She hadn't slept at all last night, come to think of it, not drunk any water this morning. She felt faint, suddenly, and sick. She would have liked to lie down here, go to sleep on the ground, but it was too hot, and she knew one ought never to go to sleep in the sun. She forced herself to get up, wandered back to the fence, sat.

She stared at the daisies, and all of a sudden it struck her that if she used to bring Mama daisies for her birthday – then her birthday must be now. Daisies only bloom at a certain time of the year, which meant that Mama's birthday fell when the daisies bloomed, which meant that it was now. She grew confused trying to work it out. Her head ached and she felt dizzy. Everything shimmered before her eyes, the fence and fields and flowers seemed to be shrouded in a yellow haze, like a picture behind coloured glass. Then the picture cleared and it was no longer a field but a small colourful garden. A path led from the gate to an ivy-grown pavilion, and masses of flowers grew on both sides of the path – all kinds of flowers, in every shape and colour, and each had a name of its own. And over there by the fence were the white daisies on their tall, straight, easy-to-pick stems and Biba was picking a bunch.

Then the garden turned back into fields-behind-barbed-wire again, and she felt sick and wanted to get up but didn't have the strength. She gazed straight ahead of her – not in order to see anything, not in order to call back the picture, but just because she mustn't close her eyes or she'd be dizzy again. Mama's voice came back insistently: "Don't you remember?"

And then she did. She wasn't surprised: it was almost as though she had expected it, as though some screen had suddenly lifted and there, behind it, was everything contained in Mama's "remember."

It all came rushing back:

A large old house. *Their* house. Home. A wide sweep of steps leading to a veranda with tall windows. A swing here. A door to one side, leading to the kitchen where Francka is making a cake. She has covered it in whipped cream and is now sticking candles on top. Piano music is coming from the drawing room. Papa is playing. You can tell there is going to be a party, that visitors are expected. Mama is busy preparing for them, but Biba can't wait – can't wait for Francka to finish the cake, for the visitors to turn up: she wants to give Mama her present now. She runs into the room, her arms full of the white daisies she has picked all by herself. She plants herself in front of Mama – young, beautiful, laughing Mama with her long hair loose on her shoulders, wearing a lovely new dress that makes her look prettier than ever – and recites a poem for her. Then Mama takes her hands and they waltz round the room together, laughing and singing, and Papa plays for them till he stops because he wants to join them too. Afterwards Mama takes the daisies, arranges them carefully in a bowl, and puts them in the most festive place in the room – on top of the piano.

A soldier stood before her.

She did not jump, wasn't even frightened, sat for a moment looking at his good-humoured face. She knew him: he was one of the young soldiers who had arrived here together with her. She had encountered him before at this spot – as though he, too, came here in search of his memories. Biba felt certain that he would never have come to chase her away from the fence of his own accord, but that he had been ordered to by the Soldier of the Golden Buttons and was obliged to obey. She got to her feet, sent him a mute greeting as though to convey that she understood and wasn't angry with him, and moved away.

Her pictures of the past stayed with her. She remembered it all now – the large garden surrounding their house, the meadow all about and the woodland, Papa at the pharmacy and Papa at the piano. They all seemed separate, though, single images that refused to blend into one whole pattern. The picture that recurred most often was the one of Mama: young and lovely and gay, holding the white daisies in her hand and listening to Biba's recital of the birthday poem.

How had the words gone?

"I'm a little mouse... I'm a little mouse... I'm a little mouse..."

The sand was burning under her feet, the sun hot on her neck. Her head swam. Yellow spots appeared on the sand before her, each like a small sun.

"I'm a little mouse... I'm a little mouse... I'm a little mouse..."

One of the suns became a field of daisies, but when she bent to pick them they dissolved under her fingers.

The sun burnt and blazed. She found a piece of paper, folded it into a paper hat, put it on her head, moved on.

One of the small suns at her feet began to grow. She paused, watching it expand, then shrink again, laugh at her, then frown, then split up into a thousand small suns again. She walked – trampling them – the suns, the daisies.

And there was Francka in the sun, wearing a white apron, holding a cake –

And Mama with the dishes –

And Papa at the piano –

A shadow appeared in the sand. She looked at it as at a mirage, a trick of one of the little suns, but it stayed there, did not change, did not vanish. She stepped into it, was aware of a large towering presence beside her.

A tree.

She was standing by a tall tree with thick foliage. She circled it, not daring to touch it for fear it would dissolve. Then she saw moss at its foot, and somehow the sight gave her the courage to stroke the bark and lay her cheek against it. She would have liked to stretch out here, under the tree, shaded by its branches and leaves, and fall asleep like a girl in a story.

She saw a fence – a fence made of brown wooden boards tapering to a point like a row of flat pencils. There was a little gate in the fence, too, like at home, and it seemed to open of itself as in a fairytale. She passed through, walked along the white gravel path, between beds of flowers.

The ones nearest the fences were small pinkish-violet carnations with flecked petals, emitting a strong sweetish scent. On the other side were high, thick-leafed tulips, each one a different colour. Beyond them grew bushes with fragrant white flowers, across from them some plant with red berries, and then side by side like a row of soldiers – white daisies.

"White daisies," she whispered to herself. She drew near, bent, felt the large petals caress her cheek, put out a hand but let it fall again, not to touch, not to banish this lovely dream.

She wandered back to the path, sat down, closed her eyes and breathed the flower-perfumed air. Then there was someone standing before her. Had the soldier come to chase her away again? She opened her eyes, saw a pair of boots standing on the white gravel of the path. She studied them, trying to understand why the gravel path was still there too – for if this was a soldier he ought to be standing on sand. She felt puzzled and vaguely perturbed. It was beginning to dawn on her that this was no dream, that she was in a real garden with real flowers, with a white gravel path and a fence of flat pencils and a tree, a real tree, solid and shade-giving. She looked at it all through her eyelashes, afraid to raise her eyes, sensing the looming menace above her.

A calm male voice make her jump:

"Hello, pretty girl!"
She looked up, froze.
It was he – the Soldier with the Golden Buttons.

She scrambled to her feet, fully awake now. It came to her in a flash that something terrible must have happened, though she couldn't quite make out how or what. All she knew for the moment was that she was here alone, face to face with the Soldier with the Golden Buttons. But where? Where was she?

And then she understood. The sign!

She had passed the sign warning off trespassers. Like the boy whose dead body had been exhibited one day during roll-call.

She clung to the fence, stood there as though waiting for the firing-squad.

"How nice of you to come and visit me."

A shiver ran down her spine.

"We're old friends, aren't we?"

She cast a swift look about her. The gate was too far – she'd never make it. And anyhow, it was madness to think she could take even one step without his permission or command. She hunched her shoulders, waited.

"Come, my little pretty, come!"

No, no point of even thinking of flight. She was in his hands. She would have to do whatever he told her.

He motioned her towards the house, and she obeyed, dazed with fear, expecting the worst. His hand on her shoulder was like a touch of live coal. She walked along the white gravel path, reached the house.

The Soldier with the Golden Buttons opened the door, told her to enter. She moved, crossed the threshold, recoiled: eight pairs of boots stood before her, eight figures in trim uniforms, eight soldiers with golden buttons. They were all smiling politely.

"Gentlemen," the Soldier with the Golden Buttons announced solemnly, emphasizing each word, "as you see, this young lady has come to honour us with her presence. I hope you will receive her with all the attention due to her."

The officers all bowed correctly.

"She is very welcome!" said the fat officer, the one who had taken the Big Girl away.

Biba wondered whether she ought to say something in reply, but waited to be told.

"And what is the young lady's name?" one officer asked, thrusting his face close to hers.

"Biba," she whispered hoarse with fright.

"Biba!" – he sounded amused - "Did you hear that? Biba!"

They all laughed as though she had said something terribly funny.

"Biba is a very pretty name," declared one officer, stroking her hair. She bore it bravely without blinking an eyelid. "I've a little girl called Biba myself," he added.

"Right, gentlemen," the Soldier with the Golden Buttons said, "Dinner!"

"I hope," he added, turning to Biba, "that you won't refuse to join us at the table, young lady.'

He gave her a little bow, and with his hand on her shoulder led her towards a door at the end of the corridor.

Biba walked, her eyes on the door wide with alarm. She could hear the tinkle of glass beyond it. What was happening in the room? What would they do to her in there? She reached the door, stopped in her tracks.

The Soldier with the Golden Buttons made an inviting gesture, but Biba did not move. The officers behind her had stopped, too, as though waiting for their "young lady" to lead the way, but Biba stayed where she was, cold with terror. What awaited her there? The Soldier with the Golden Buttons gave her a slight push and she stumbled forward – a step, another, and she was there.

The first thing that met her eye was a festively laid table; a white table-cloth, plates, shining silver, tall sparkling glasses, a basket filled with fresh fragrant bread, carafes with iced water, bowls of fruit.

Laughing and chattering, the officers moved to their places, remained standing behind their chairs, waiting for Biba to be seated first. Only the Soldier with the Golden Buttons stayed beside Biba.

"Well," he said, "how do you like it? We prepared it all specially for you."

Biba continued looking at the table, dry-mouthed with fear, and with a sudden overwhelming thirst.

"That is your place, over there," he said, and led her to the head of the table.

The chair was too high for Biba, and so was the table: only her nose peeped out over it as she sat. They all burst into loud laughter at the sight – and their laughter was so frank, so cheerful, that Biba found herself laughing with them.

And now even her fright was beginning to leave her. Here she was, after all, sitting at a richly laid table, and here were these officers, all pleasant and cheerful as though hers really was nothing but a friendly visit.

Someone brought a big cushion and placed it on Biba's chair and now she was higher than them.

"All she needs is a crown on her head!"

Her fear was all gone. She sat very straight, trying to live up to the occasion, even appear a little ladylike to them. They seemed so changed – not like officers at all.. The napkins they had tucked in under their chins covered part of their uniforms, their boots were invisible under the table, they had removed their belts and caps. She saw them with different eyes because they were different. They were kind and they liked her. They must like her, mustn't they, if they had invited her to their table, and if one of them even had a girl of his own called Biba.

"So how's our little princess?"

Biba smiled, pleased, thanking them with her eyes for being so nice to her. She looked at the carafe in front of her and longed to drink some water. A hand came over the table, lifted the carafe and poured water into a glass. Biba's eyes followed, stared at the clear jet filling the glass, at the ice-cubes floating on top, and her thirst grew. She considered holding up her glass to be filled, but thought she had better do nothing without being told. She would wait till they offered her some.

The officers straightened their napkins, played with their

spoons, nibbled bread, drank water, waited. The door on the far side of the room facing Biba, opened, and a soldier came through. He bore a tray high over his head, and on the tray a large china soup tureen emitting a mouthwatering smell. Biba's hands stirred restlessly on the table. The smell had bowled her over completely. She readied her plate. The soldier began to serve the soup, starting at Biba's left, moving round the table back to her.

She looked at him expectantly, grateful in advance, but he only lifted the tureen from the tray, put it on the table right before Biba, and went out. She followed him with her eyes, stunned, puzzled. Maybe he had forgotten something and would be back in a minute? She looked at the door that had closed being him, then at the officers. They were all eating. The door stayed shut, the soup tureen stood on the table, everyone had been served and only Biba's plate remained empty.

Had they forgotten her?

She looked left and right at her table neighbors, but no one took notice of her, no one even glanced her way. What should she do? She watched the golden-yellow dumplings swimming about the soup, bumping against the little squares of carrot, the green and spices whose lovely smell filled the room. The tureen stood beside Biba's place, covering its edge with steam.

Perhaps they meant her to help herself? That was it! Why hadn't she thought of it before? Of course she shouldn't have expected to be served like one of the officers. She was supposed to serve herself. That no doubt was why they had left the tureen so near her – so she would be able to reach it.

She glanced round the table again, trying to make sure that she wasn't about to do something she mustn't, then raised herself slightly in her chair and put out a hand. Her hand shook a little at the thought that in a minute she would have some of this delicious soup on her plate, would bring a spoonful of it to her mouth. Tingling with excitement she looked at the officers once more. They were all busy, bent over their plates. She reached the soup ladle, and just then an officer's hand came out of nowhere and removed the tureen.

When the tureen returned it was empty. Biba slumped in her seat, trying to make herself small, to hide. But in a moment, conscious of being among officers, of being supposed to do only what was expected of her, she collected herself. No doubt she had acted wrongly and they punished her by taking the soup away. She mustn't do anything without being told, without being given express permission.

She was thirsty. She was growing thirstier by the minute, and only now she saw that her glass had disappeared. She watched the carafe. The ice had nearly melted: only two tiny slivers were still floating in there. She stared at them till they, too, were gone, then looked at the officers again. They were finishing their soup. Maybe they hadn't given her any because there hadn't been enough to go round? Ah, but in that case they would surely let her have some of the second course.

But then the second course came and Biba's plate remained empty. Dry-mouthed she watched the soldier refill the carafe, splashing a few drops of water on her sweaty forehead as he dropped the ice-cubes in; yearningly, she watched them start to melt again. If she could just wet her lips!

The tureen had been replaced by a bowl of lettuce. She inhaled the sharp vinegar smell till her jaws ached with it, gazed at the crisp green lettuce leaves and felt her mouth shrivel. She heard them pour water into their glasses, saw them cut the meat, saw the vinegar dripping from the lettuce leaves, saw and heard their teeth chewing the food, saw them dip their bread in gravy, stick their forks into the brown-crusted pastry, wipe their chins with their napkins.

And the smells of all the dishes before her mingled and became one great agony – a pain that twisted her stomach and seared her lips. She felt faint, wanted to rest her head on the table and sleep. She was beginning to grow muddled, unable to think, knowing only that she was thirsty, so thirsty – that she would collapse if she couldn't at least wet her lips.

Her eyes went to the carafe. She wanted to jump up, seize it in both hands, hide under the table with it and drink and drink and drink, no matter what happened after. But as she looked the carafe seemed to recede, to grow smaller and smaller as it moved away and out of her reach.

The door opened again: the soldier with the tray, and on it a single plate – large and quite empty.

Breathlessly she watched his progress.

He approached the table, put down the tray, and started moving from one officer to the next, emptying the food remnants onto the big plate in his hand – starting down the table from Biba's left, then crossing to the other side.

Biba revived.

"That's for me. That must be for me," she told herself.

"Of course! How could I think they would let me eat with them, eat of the same dishes. They are officers! But it doesn't matter, it doesn't matter at all, just so long as they'll let me have something at last. It isn't unclean or anything – it's what they left on their plates – they didn't touch it – it's clean – sure it is - yes, yes, here he is coming now. Oh, what a lot of food he's got there! Now, he'll give me some water, too, no doubt. Maybe the whole carafe..."

The soldier approached slowly. Biba sat up, fidgeted in her chair, started to push away to make room but relented, not sure she was allowed to do that. And she wouldn't do anything to risk being punished again. Not now!

She kept her eyes on the soldier's plate, already imagining the taste of each scrap of food on it, its feel in her mouth...

The soldier was standing before her. He moved to hand her the plate – but slowly, holding it high in the air above her with his eyes on her face. Biba met his glance. She knew him and smiled. He seemed uneasy, trying to avoid her eyes. She knew him: he belonged to the same group as the soldier by the fence. Only what was he keeping that plate up there over her head when he must know how hungry she was? She grew nervous. The soldier lowered the plate till it was nearly before her, then turned abruptly and went out.

"No!" she shrieked, and her hands flew out after him.

A great burst of laughter roused her. Startled, she put her hand to her mouth to stifle the cry escaping her. Stony with horror, she looked at the fat faces round the table, fat lips roaring with laughter.

"She's caught on at last!"

Biba sat. The cushion had slipped to the floor but she took no notice. Her face hurt, and her lips were so dry that she dared not open them for fear they would bleed. She bowed her head, unwilling to let them see the tears she could no longer hold back.

The officers went on laughing wiping their lips, dabbing at their eyes with their napkins.

"Congratulations! That really was brilliant!"

"It always works best with children. You've got to catch their imagination, gain their confidence – and then you can do what you like with them," the Soldier with the Golden Buttons was explaining. He lighted a cigarette, sat back satisfied.

"Still, it needs quite a bit of patience, what?"

"Did you see how she was hoping, she'd at least get the scraps?"

"She didn't give up hope till the very end!"

They poured drinks, peeled fruit, smoked, tittered, looked at Biba, nudged each other, whispered, giggled, drank each other's health.

The Soldier with the Golden Buttons sat quietly smoking and watching Biba thoughtfully. He looked as pleased as someone after a great victory who expects to be praised and flattered.

An idea seemed to cross his mind. He tapped his glass to draw the other's attention, and when they fell silent he said softly pensively:

"I'm willing to bet that she's still hoping."

"Impossible!"

"After all this?"

"I don't believe it."

"I do!"

"So do I!"

"Come over here, everybody!" the Soldier with the Golden Buttons called.

Chairs scraped as they rose, moved, whispering.

Biba remained alone at the head of the table, her eyes lowered, the tears running down her face, dripping onto the empty plate before her. Their whispers reached her through the buzzing in her ears, but she couldn't make out what they were saying. She was thinking of only one thing now, the half cup of water waiting for her in the hut. How long would it be till they let her go? Why couldn't they at least allow her to leave now? What were they waiting for? Why wouldn't they let her go?

The officers came out of their huddle, returned to their places by the table, stood behind their chairs like before, when they had waited for Biba to sit down first. They called the soldier, and he went and came back with his tray. The Soldier with the Golden Buttons took things from it, arranged them on the table, stood back eyeing the effect, then shifted an object or two as though wishing everything to be just right. At last he turned to Biba:

"Come, little one, come here!"

His voice seemed to reach her from a great distance, deep and booming as though from a well, that last word echoing and re-echoing. She looked up and her head swam. Everything seemed to move before her eyes – the long table, the fat figures behind it, the big hands that were approaching her now, growing and growing like the hands of the man-eating giant who took little dwarves from their beds and ate them up. She blinked, trying to get things into focus. The hands were still there. They belonged to the Soldier with the Golden Buttons.

"Come, Biba, come!" he called.

She wanted to move but couldn't. He took a step nearer, and she sensed the threat in his manner. She tried to get up again but her chair was too close to the table.

Someone pulled the chair back for her. She got up.

"Come here!" he said, his voice stricter, but still polite.

Slowly she walked over the soft carpet, halted when he told her. Now she was surrounded by boots again, by officers in uniforms and belts and revolvers. That was how they looked when they turned up for roll-call, with such grins on their faces had they taken away the Big Girl and the girl who wouldn't beat her mother and the dead boy's body. She was ready to obey their commands.

The officer who had a girl like Biba stepped forward, sat on his heels before her.

"Look, Biba," he said, "see these plates on the table here? Well, each plate contains one of the dishes we've had for dinner today." He was speaking slowly, taking his time, making sure she understood. "Now, there's only just one thing on each plate – a piece of meat, a slice of bread, some lettuce, and so on. You can look at it all, and then you can choose one single dish."

Biba waited for him to say what he had to say, her eyes on his face. She was watching him calmly, even a bit pertly, as if he weren't an officer at all.

The Soldier with the Golden Buttons asked: "Did you understand that? From all you see on the table here you can take one – but only one! You are to *choose*."

She raised her head and slowly, lifted her eyes, looked straight into his. Her eyes did not waver. For the first time she stood before him with her back straight and her head erect – unafraid. She looked at him calmly, with dignity, with a smile on her lips – the way he had looked at her the first time. It came to her that she had waited a long time for this moment, and she was glad that it had come and that she had had the courage to meet its challenge.

He threw his head back as though to remove a strand of hair from his forehead, and a nerve by his mouth began to twitch. He glanced round uneasily, checking to see if the others had noticed the sudden difference that had come over Biba, his own nervousness. Yet he wouldn't give up so soon, spoke again, controlling his voice:

"Whatever you choose will be yours. Look, there's water here too – you may drink a whole glass!"

Biba looked at the glass. Her parched mouth opened slightly but her arms remained stiffly by her sides. Motionless she gazed at the table, at the plates, the food, the water – and they all seemed unreal, like pictures in the sand that would dissolve at a touch.

She looked beyond the line-up dishes and saw a vase filled with daisies, the large white petals towering majestically over the range of plates: an island of reality.

She kept her eyes on the flowers, and they shone with all that was absent from this room – light and space and warmth and beauty – and filled her with a marvelous sense of having something that was hers alone.

An idea struck her. She would take a daisy. Yes, she would take a single white daisy. They had said she could take what she wanted from the table – then why not a daisy? It was the only thing she truly wanted.

She glanced at the officers, then back at the vase. Yes, she would do it. No doubt they'd be stunned. They, no doubt, thought she had difficulty choosing a dish because she wanted them all. But she would let everything stand and take just one white daisy, and walk past all the boots, through the garden, past the tree, across all the small suns in the sand – walk all aglow with the splendour of her flower, walk through the camp, past all the huts, past all the beds, till she came to the bed where he mother lay and only there she would stop. She would stand before her, hold out the flower, and say:

"Happy birthday, Mama!"

And Mama would take the flower, smell it, and its smell would bring back the colour to her cheeks, the strength to her limbs, and she would recover like in that story about the boy and the heart...

"Well, what's up?" the voice of the Soldier with the Golden Buttons woke her from her trance. He turned her roughly towards him. "Do you want something or don't you?"

"Yes, I do!" she replied firmly.

She looked at him fearlessly. There was nothing he could do to her any longer. He had lost his power over her, and he knew it. She looked at the others and they grew uneasy under her gaze and averted their eyes.

Biba moved to the table and the flowers seemed to beckon her on. She could already picture Mama standing there, gay and happy, her long hair loose on her shoulders, her face flushed with pleasure, impatient for Biba to get through her birthday poem so they could dance through the room together.

Her hand reached for the flower – and then another picture formed in her mind, a picture of Mama as she was today, now, there in the laundry hut – bowed, thin, her face old and gray and lifeless, her shaking hands holding a piece of bread and bringing it carefully to her mouth crumb by crumb... This picture was here, alive and real before her eyes.

She turned her eyes away from the flowers, searched among the plates for a slice of bread, found it – a thick slice, big as three-days' ration. She knew she was about to do what the officers expected she would, knew she was giving them one more reason for laughter, for triumph – but she also knew it was bread her mother needed. She put out a hand and took it, turned on her heel and moved to the door. She walked between the two rows of black boots, out of the room, over the white gravel path, past the sign with its warning – and the officers' laughter followed her. But Biba heard nothing. She reached the laundry, peered through the keyhole, and when she saw that Mama was still there she leaned against the blazing wall of the hut and waited, the bread in her hand like a flower, her lips whispering:

"I'm a little mouse... a little mouse..."

But try as she would, she could not remember the rest of the poem.